SOFTWARE GUIDE

Using VP-Expert

Ernest S. Colantonio

University of Illinois

D. C. HEATH AND COMPANY

Lexington, Massachusetts Toronto

Photo Credits

Figures 1.2, 1.3, 1.7, and 1.8(d) courtesy of International Business Machines Corp.
Figure 1.4 courtesy of Intel.
Figure 1.5 courtesy of Memorex.
Figure 1.6 courtesy of Seagate Technologies.
Figures 1.10(b) and 1.11 courtesy of Hewlett Packard.

IBM PC is a registered trademark of International Business Machines Corporation.
VP-Expert is a trademark and Paperback Software is registered trademark of Paperback Software International, Berkeley, CA, USA.

Published simultaneously in Canada.

Printed in the United States of America.

International Standard Book Number: 0-669-19957-5

10 9 8 7 6 5 4 3 2 1

Preface

In this day and age, it's become increasingly evident that a truly general education must include some exposure to computers. Fortunately, microcomputers have become so inexpensive that literally millions of them have surfaced in homes, schools, offices, and businesses everywhere. What's more, they're being used by people from all walks of life.

For most of us, being able to use a computer for daily tasks means first learning to use its operating system to some extent. Most users then master some type of application software, such as a word processing, spreadsheet, or data base management package. Many people continue to study more advanced or specialized software. One of today's most exciting microcomputer applications is the expert system shell, a software package that uses the techniques of artificial intelligence to help users solve problems, make decisions, and obtain advice.

The Purpose of this Guide

This software guide can be used for self-study or in any introductory class that teaches the use of these two specific types of software:

1. IBM PC-DOS or MS-DOS
2. VP-Expert

Its lessons teach the student, with a hands-on, step-by-step approach, how to apply these software packages to everyday tasks. For the greatest understanding, students should follow the guide as they run DOS on their own (or their school's or employer's) computer. On completion of the lessons, the student will be amply prepared to use DOS and VP-Expert for common applications.

The Software

The *Software Guide* teaches the use of the world's most popular microcomputer operating system and expert system shell. Although neither PC-DOS nor MS-DOS is included with this guide, a copy of this operating system is usually purchased as standard equipment with most IBM and IBM-compatible microcomputers. The most recent educational version of the Paperback Software program VP-Expert is available with this guide.

PC-DOS and MS-DOS 3.30

Almost identical, these twins are the *de facto* standard operating system used on the IBM family of personal computers and compatible machines. Since everyone who uses one of these computers must deal with the operating system to some extent, DOS tops the list of important software to become familiar with. Most of the DOS commands covered in this guide also work with all versions of DOS 2.00 and higher, including IBM DOS 4.00.

VP-Expert Version 2.0

Paperback Software's VP-Expert is an expert system development tool. It helps you build complete, functional computer programs to give advice, make diagnoses, or solve problems in a specific field. Unlike traditional artificial intelligence programming languages such as LISP and PROLOG, VP-Expert is easy to learn and simple to apply. Using VP-Expert is an ideal way for beginners to learn about artificial intelligence and expert systems.

VP-Expert's Features

- Menu-driven user interface
- Extensive, built-in help facilities
- Built-in text editor
- Simple, English-like commands
- Full use of color displays
- Backward chaining inference engine for problem solving
- Development windows for observing the problem-solving process
- Confidence factors for uncertain information
- Commands for explaining and graphing the logic of a consultation
- Automatic creation of an expert system from a table of facts
- Automatic question generation
- Rapid execution of programs

System Requirements

- An IBM or IBM-compatible microcomputer
- MS- or PC-DOS Version 2.0 or higher
- At least 384K RAM
- An 80-column monochrome or color monitor
- Two 5¼-inch or 3½-inch floppy disk drives, or at least one floppy disk drive and a hard disk drive

Limitations of the Educational Version of VP-Expert

The educational version of VP-Expert contains the following limitations when compared to the Professional version of the program:

1. The maximum size of a rule base is 16K.
2. A maximum of three rule bases may be chained together. On the attempt of a third chain command (to access a fourth rule base) an error message appears and the job is terminated. You will be returned to DOS.
3. The maximum number of data base file records which can be read is 150. An error message will inform you if you attempt too many data base accesses.

The Guide

The *Software Guide* is both a user's manual and a workbook with exercises. It is specifically designed to be used with DOS and VP-Expert. This guide, which consists of three parts, covers

1. An introduction to microcomputers
2. DOS instructions and exercises
3. VP-Expert instructions and exercises

As a user's manual, the *Software Guide* provides an introduction to the software, a description of its general features, and a series of lessons on how to use these features. As a workbook, the *Software Guide* gives students clear explanations, step-by-step instructions, and plenty of exercises to practice and test their skills. More specifically, its offerings include:

- Clear learning objectives for each part
- A description of the software's general capabilities
- Carefully paced step-by-step lessons
- Over 100 exercises ranging in difficulty from simple to complex
- Numerous examples
- Answers to multiple choice and fill-in exercises
- Command summaries for DOS and VP-Expert for easy reference
- A comprehensive glossary
- Exceptionally clear, actual screen views

The *Software Guide* can be assigned in a class or used in a self-paced lab setting. Either way, the workbook and accompanying software help students get the operating system and expert system experience they'll need in today's world.

Acknowledgments

Several people were involved in making this project possible. I am especially grateful to Lee Ripley and Pam Kirshen for the original inception of the idea for this guide's predecessors. Their help and support, along with that of Jill Hobbs, was greatly appreciated. Special thanks go to C. Brian Honess of the University of South Carolina for many of the short and long problems that were adapted from the original *Software Guide*. I'd like to thank Peter Gordon of D. C. Heath for his new vision of what these manuals could become, and Kitty Sheehan and Kathy Savage for handling all of those little details, as well as Cia Boynton, Anne Starr, and Irene Cinelli for all the time and effort they contributed toward the completion of this project.

E. S. C.

Contents

1

The Microcomputer

Learning Objectives

After reading this chapter, you should know the following:

- What is meant by the term *microcomputer*
- The basic operations performed by all computers
- The four major hardware components of a typical microcomputer system
- The major components inside a microcomputer's system unit
- The three major types of microcomputer displays
- How the various special-purpose keys on a microcomputer keyboard are used
- The four most popular types of microcomputer printers
- The three major categories of microcomputer software
- How to turn on a microcomputer
- How to operate a microcomputer printer
- How to care for floppy disks

Introduction

We begin this first chapter by introducing IBM and IBM-compatible microcomputers, their hardware components, and popular types of software. (By *IBM-compatible* we mean any computer that works like a comparable IBM model and can run the same software.) Then we discuss a few helpful hints for working with microcomputers.

What Is a Microcomputer?

Its very name tells us that a **microcomputer** is a small computer, and a **computer** is an electronic device that performs calculations and processes data. Most people think of a microcomputer as being small enough to fit on top of a desk. Although some powerful models can serve several users simultaneously, most microcomputers are used by only one person at a time. For this reason, microcomputers are also often called **personal computers**.

Another characteristic of microcomputers is that their "brain" or **central processing unit (CPU)** consists of a single electronic device known as a **microprocessor**. This device, a marvel of miniature engineering, controls the microcomputer, performs its calculations, and processes data. A microprocessor is just one type of integrated circuit chip, which is a thin slice of semiconductor material, such as pure silicon crystal, impregnated with carefully selected impurities. These chips are commonly used in computers and many other modern electronic devices.

One way to define microcomputers is by what they do. They can be used to help accomplish many different tasks. At the lowest level, however, a microcomputer performs the same basic operations as all computers. This can be summed up as *input*, *processing*, and *output* (see Figure 1.1).

Figure 1.1 What a Computer Does

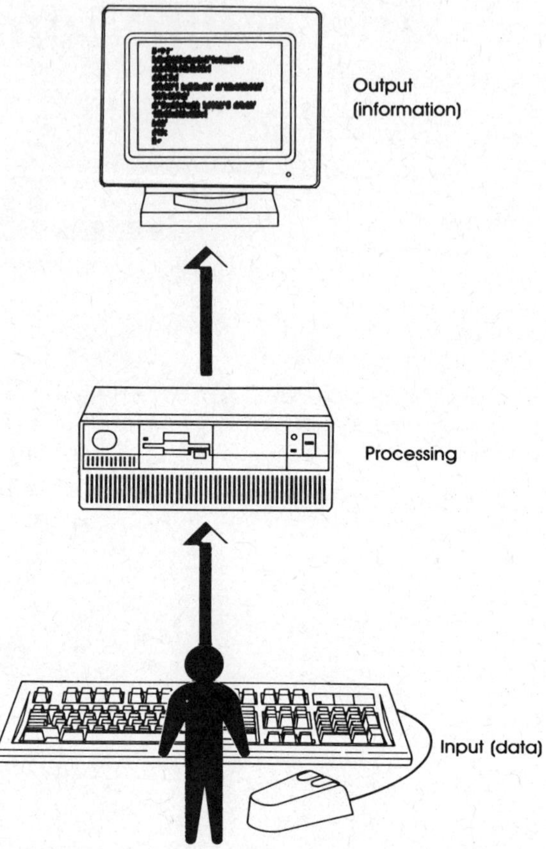

First, a **program** is needed to tell the computer what to do. This is a set of instructions that controls a computer's operation. The program lets you enter raw **data**, which can consist of numbers, text, pictures, and even sounds. These data entered into the computer are called **input**. The program instructs the computer to process the data by doing calculations, comparisons, and other manipulations. The final result is processed data or **information**, hopefully a more organized and useful form of the original input. This information produced by the computer is called **output**. Keep in mind that there is no magic here—a program is needed to tell the computer what to do and the output information is only as valid as the original input data.

Although microcomputers perform the same basic operations as larger computers, they differ in speed and capacity. Larger computers can generally process data faster than microcomputers. They can also internally store more data at a time than microcomputers. These factors make larger computers better for performing lots of extremely complex and time-consuming computations. Microcomputers are also less adept than larger computers at handling several different users or tasks at the same time. On the other hand, microcomputers are superbly adapted to help with many work-a-day tasks like typing papers, figuring taxes, maintaining mailing lists, sending messages, drawing charts, managing finances, and even playing games.

Finally, microcomputers generally fall within a given price range. This range varies from little as $100 to as much as $15,000. Today the average price of a typical microcomputer used in business is around $2500. This is, however, a good deal less than the cost of much more powerful computers, which may run into many thousands or millions of dollars. Although microcomputers are by no means cheap, their prices have been generally dropping even as their capabilities have increased. For example, in late 1983 the list price of a basic IBM Personal Computer XT was $5675. The list price of its successor, a similarly-equipped IBM Personal System/2 Model 30, was only $2545 when first released in mid 1987. Even though the newer Model 30 costs less than half as much as the old XT, it still has more than twice the speed and storage capacity, along with many other improvements.

Hardware

The **hardware** of a computer system is the electronic and mechanical equipment that make it work. Like a stereo system, microcomputer hardware generally consists of several distinct components connected by cables. Although there are several possible arrangements and many different models, Figure 1.2 shows a typical microcomputer system, the IBM Personal System/2 Model 50, which has four major parts: a system unit, display, keyboard, and printer. You will also notice, in this figure, a power switch, a floppy disk drive, and a mouse, all of which will be discussed later.

Figure 1.2 A Microcomputer System

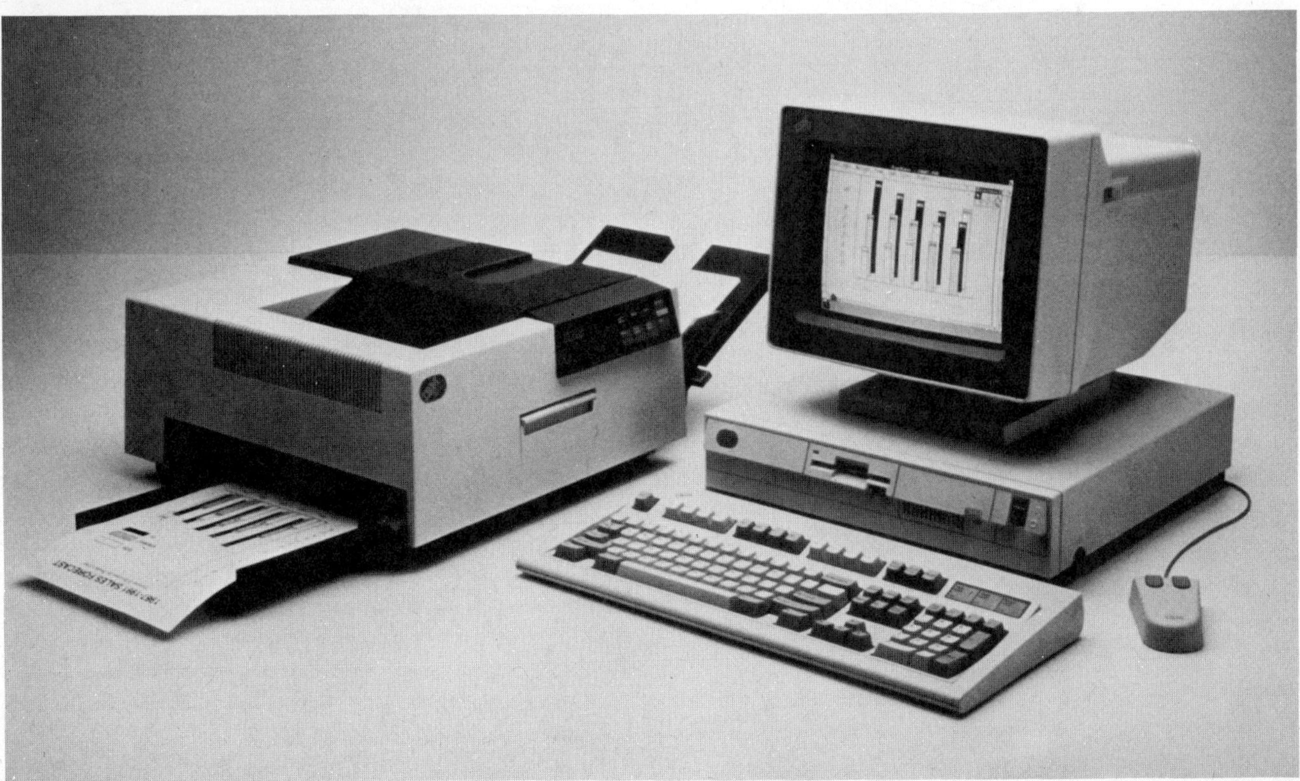

System Unit

From the outside, the system unit looks like a shallow box about the size of a portable typewriter. Figure 1.3 shows what the system unit of an IBM Personal System/2 Model 50 looks like on the inside. This central component houses important elements such as the computer's motherboard, microprocessor, memory, disk drives, and power supply.

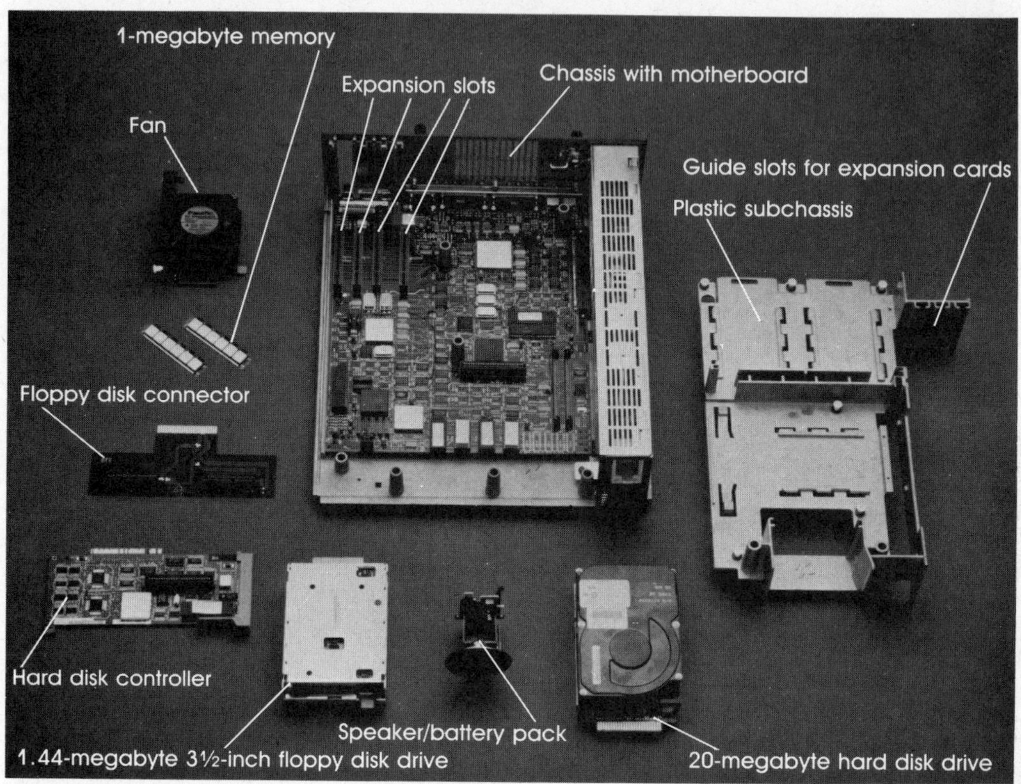

Figure 1.3 Inside the System Unit

Motherboard

The main circuit board of a computer is called the **motherboard** or **system board** (see Figure 1.4). Among other components, the motherboard holds the computer's CPU, some memory, and much of its control circuitry. In addition, the motherboard contains the **bus**, a set of wires and connectors that link the CPU to memory and other computer components.

In most microcomputers, the bus is accessible through a series of **expansion slots**. Each expansion slot is an internal connector that allows you to plug an additional circuit board into the motherboard. The IBM Personal System/2 Model 50, for example, has four expansion slots, which can be seen in Figure 1.4. Some computers come with eight or more expansion slots. A circuit board that plugs into an expansion slot is called an **expansion board, card,** or **adapter**. Such circuit boards make it possible to connect a wide variety of extra equipment to a computer, thus *expanding* its capability.

The motherboard or expansion boards also contain device controllers. A **device controller** is a set of chips or a circuit board that operates a piece of computer equipment such as a disk drive, display, keyboard, mouse, or printer. Recently, there has been a trend toward building device controllers onto microcomputer motherboards. The IBM Personal System/2 Model 50 shown in Figure 1.4, for example, has most of its device controllers on the motherboard.

Figure 1.4
A Motherboard or System Board

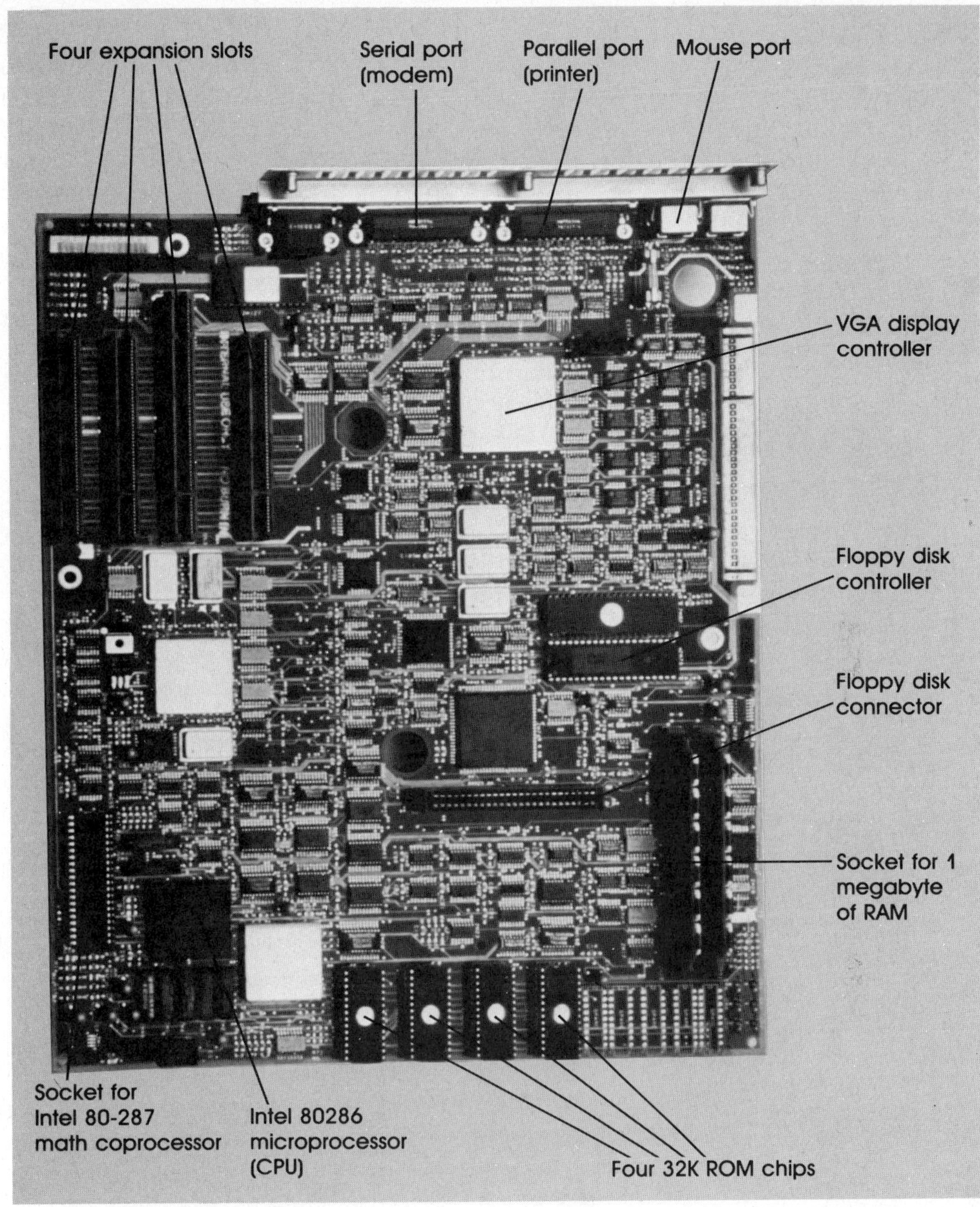

Microprocessor

As we said, the microprocessor is a microcomputer's central processing unit (CPU). It consists of a single integrated circuit chip that is usually soldered or plugged into a socket on the motherboard (see Figure 1.4). IBM and IBM-compatible microcomputers use microprocessors from the Intel 8088 family, which includes the 8088, 8086, 80286, and 80386 chips. The 8088 is used in older IBM and IBM-compatibles such as the original IBM Personal Computer and PC/XT. The slightly more efficient 8086 chip is used in IBM's newer low-end models, such as the IBM Personal System/2 Models 25 and 30. The more powerful 80286 chip is used in mid-range microcomputers, such as the original IBM Personal Computer AT and the newer IBM Personal System/2 Models 50 and 60. Finally, the very powerful and fast 80386 chip is used in high-end models, such as the IBM Personal System/2 Models 70 and 80.

Memory

Memory is a computer's internal storage, used to hold programs and data. Also called **primary storage**, memory is measured in bytes. A **byte** is the amount of storage needed to hold a single character, such as the letter A. Since computers can store many thousands or millions of bytes, the terms **kilobyte (K)** and **megabyte (M)** are often used. One kilobyte or 1K is equal to 1024 bytes. One megabyte or 1M is equal to 1,048,576 bytes. In general, microcomputer memory is made up of two types of integrated circuit chips: RAM and ROM.

RAM, which stands for **Random Access Memory**, is temporary storage. Programs and data can be stored there while they are being used and then overwritten by other programs and data later. When the computer is turned off, RAM loses its contents. Most microcomputers can now have at least 640K of RAM on their motherboards. Many can have much more installed on expansion boards. For example, the IBM Personal System/2 Model 80 can be equipped with up to 16 megabytes of RAM.

ROM, which stands for **Read Only Memory**, is permanent storage. The contents of ROM chips, which are encoded at the factory, remain intact when the computer is turned off. The programs and data permanently stored in ROM can be read and used, but never erased, changed, or augmented. Many microcomputers use ROM to store programs and data that are used frequently but need never be changed, such as portions of the operating system. Most microcomputers contain at least one ROM chip as part of their primary storage. The IBM Personal System/2 Model 50, for example, uses four 32K ROM chips on the motherboard to store essential programs and data (see Figure 1.4).

Disk Drives

A **disk drive** is a piece of equipment that can read and write programs and data on magnetic disks. A **magnetic disk** is a semi-permanent storage medium that can be erased and rewritten many times. Most microcomputers can now be equipped with two basic kinds of disk drives: floppy disk drives and hard disk drives.

A **floppy disk drive** works with **floppy disks** (also called **diskettes**), which are inexpensive, flexible magnetic disks encased in plastic (see Figure 1.5). Floppy disks can be inserted and removed from their disk drives. The IBM Personal System/2 Model 50, for example, accepts a 3½-inch diskette, which can hold up to 1.44 megabytes of programs and data. Although most newer microcomputers now come with 3½-inch disk drives, many microcomputers still use 5¼-inch floppy disk

Figure 1.5 Floppy Disks

drives. A typical 5¼-inch floppy disk holds 360K, but there are some drives that use 5¼-inch disks that hold 1.2 megabytes.

A **hard disk drive** uses one or more magnetic metal platters to hold programs and data (see Figure 1.6). Most hard disk drives have their magnetic disks permanently sealed inside. These disks are rigid, much faster, and have much greater capacity than floppy disks. Hard disk drives come in sizes ranging from 10 megabytes to several hundred megabytes. The most popular sizes are now 20, 30, and 40 megabytes. The IBM Personal System/2 Model 50, for example, comes standard with a 20 megabyte internal hard disk. On a microcomputer with a hard disk, programs are usually run from the hard disk. The floppy disk drive is generally relegated to copying software to or from the hard disk and making backup copies of important programs and data.

Figure 1.6 Hard Disk Drive

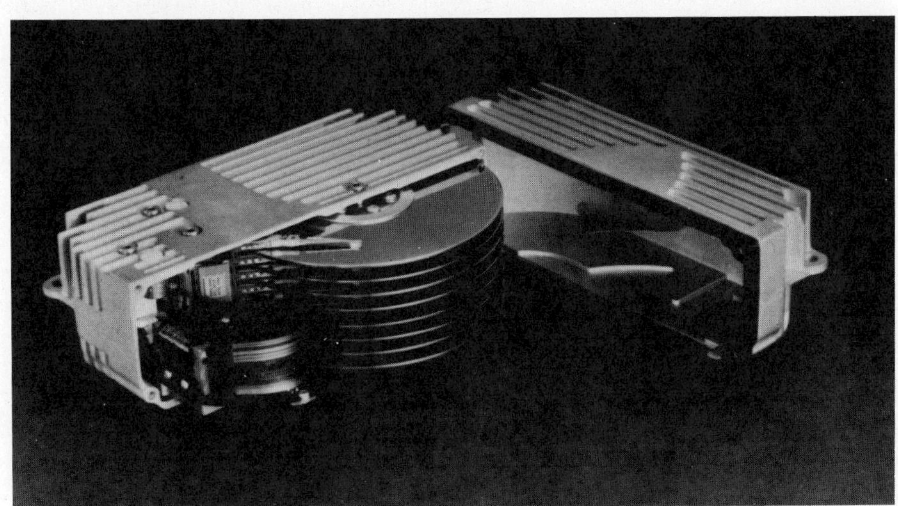

Display

A display, also called a **monitor**, is similar in many ways to an ordinary television screen. The display is used to present text and **graphics**, which are simply any kind of pictures, drawings, charts, or plots. The vast majority of computer monitors create text and graphics on the screen with tiny dots called **pixels** (short for picture elements). The number and size of these pixels determine a monitor's sharpness or **resolution**. There are three basic types of displays:

- **Monochrome Text** These monitors can only display letters, numbers, punctuation, and a limited set of other symbols in just one color, usually green on black, amber on black, white on black, or black on white.
- **Monochrome Graphics** In addition to text, these monitors can also display graphics on the screen. Only one color can be presented, but different shades of that color may be used.
- **Color Graphics** These monitors can display text and graphics in more than one color.

The capabilities of a particular display system are dependent on both the monitor itself and its device controller. The device controller for the display system is called a **display adapter**. For IBM and IBM-compatible microcomputers, there are several different display adapters that can be used. Some of these follow.

- **Monochrome Display Adapter (MDA)** This is the controller used with early low-end IBM microcomputers. It can only display text on a monochrome screen, but it generates very crisp, easy to read characters.
- **Color Graphics Adapter (CGA)** This is IBM's first microcomputer color graphics adapter. It can do color graphics, but the quality is rather poor. In other words, its low resolution makes text and graphics look rather fuzzy. Furthermore, the CGA is limited to a maximum of only 16 different colors, of which only only four can be on the screen at the same time.
- **Hercules Graphics Adapter** This adapter, made by Hercules Computer Technology, acts as a monochrome display adapter, but adds monochrome graphics capability.
- **Enhanced Graphics Adapter (EGA)** This color graphics adapter from IBM can do everything the CGA can do, yet is much better than the CGA. The resolution is significantly higher and the maximum number of different colors on the screen is 16 out of 64 possible choices.
- **Multi-Color Graphics Array (MCGA)** This is the display adapter built onto the motherboards of the IBM Personal System/2 Models 25 and 30. It can be used with either a monochrome graphics or color graphics monitor. It's maximum resolution is better than the EGA and can display a maximum of 256 different colors on the screen at once out of 262,144 possible choices.
- **Video Graphics Array (VGA)** This is the display adapter built onto the motherboards of the IBM Personal System/2 Models 50, 60, 70, and 80. It can also be purchased as a separate expansion board for other types of IBM and IBM-compatible computers. Slightly more advanced than the MCGA, the VGA can also do everything the EGA can do.

Keyboard

The keyboard is the primary device for entering text and telling the computer what to do. It is similar, in many respects, to a typewriter keyboard. Many microcomputers also have an auxiliary input device known as a **mouse**. This little box, which is glided across the table top, allows the user to manipulate objects on the display screen and select actions to be performed by pressing one or more buttons.

For IBM and IBM-compatible microcomputers, there are three basic keyboard designs. These are the original IBM Personal Computer keyboard, the original IBM Personal Computer AT keyboard, and the new IBM Enhanced Keyboard. Figure 1.7 shows all three of these keyboards. Besides the usual letters and punctuation marks that you're likely to find on any typewriter, a computer keyboard has other important keys:

- **Enter (or Return)** Analogous to the carriage return on a typewriter, this key is used to signal the end of an entry. Basically, it tells the computer to go ahead and process what was just typed.
- **Backspace** Like the Backspace key on a typewriter, this key is used to go back and type over a previously typed character.
- **Shift** Located at either side of the keyboard, one of the Shift keys is held down while pressing another key to produce a capital letter or the symbol shown on the top part of the key.
- **Caps Lock** This key is like the Caps Lock key on a typewriter, except that it works for only letter keys. When the caps lock key is pressed, capital letters will appear when you press letter keys. When Caps Lock is pressed again, small letters will appear when their keys are pressed.
- **Tab** Like the Tab key on a typewriter, this key is used to advance to the next tab stop.

Figure 1.7 (top) Original IBM PC Keyboard, (center) "AT-Style" Keyboard, and (bottom) IBM Enhanced Keyboard

- **Escape** The Escape key (abbreviated **Esc**) is often used to cancel a previously typed entry or to prematurely end a program.
- **Break** This key is very much like the Escape key and is used by some programs in a similar fashion.
- **Control** Somewhat like a Shift key, the Control key (abbreviated **Ctrl**) is pressed in conjunction with other keys. It's used to control a program's actions by sending certain codes to the computer.
- **Alternate** Very similar to the Control key, the Alternate key (abbreviated **Alt**) is also pressed in conjunction with other keys. It's used to give an alternate meaning to the keys pressed along with it.
- **Insert** This key (abbreviated **Ins**) is often used to insert a new entry between existing entries.

- **Delete** This key (abbreviated **Del**) is often used to erase an entry or a single character.
- **Function Keys** These are keys that are pressed to activate frequently used operations within a program. They are used differently by different programs. IBM-compatible keyboards have either 10 function keys along the left side or 12 function keys across the top. The function keys are labeled with an F followed by a number, like this: F1, F2, F3, etc.
- **Cursor Movement Keys** Most programs use these keys to let you move the **cursor** (a little blinking underscore or box) around the screen. In a word processing program, for example, the cursor marks the place where text is inserted, deleted, or otherwise manipulated. The cursor movement keys include Up Arrow, Down Arrow, Left Arrow, Right Arrow, Home, End, Page Up, and Page Down.
- **Numeric Keypad** This is an array of keys at the right side of a keyboard that resembles the layout of a calculator's keys. It includes the ten digits and other symbols that facilitate the entry of numbers and formulas. On the IBM PC and AT keyboards, the numeric keypad is superimposed on the cursor movement keys.
- **Num Lock** This key is used to switch the function of the numeric keypad. In one state, the numeric keypad acts as number keys. In the other state, the numeric keypad acts as cursor movement keys. You press the Num Lock key to switch between these two states.
- **Print Screen** If you have a printer, this key is pressed to send a copy of the current screen to your printer. On some keyboards, it is abbreviated **PrtSc**.
- **Pause** This key is used to temporarily suspend the operation of the current program.
- **Scroll Lock** This key is not used by very many programs and it has no standard function. Some programs use it to switch the Cursor Movement keys into a state in which they can move (or scroll) the whole screen up, down, left, or right.

Printer

A **printer** is a device used to produce permanent copies of text and possibly graphics on paper. Although a printer is not absolutely necessary to run most programs, it is an extremely useful addition to a microcomputer system. This is because computers are commonly used to produce letters, reports, books, tables, figures, charts, graphs, diagrams, maps, and pictures. Paper output, or *hard copy* as it's also called, is a convenient medium for distributing and communicating this work to others. The four kinds of printers most frequently used with microcomputers are dot-matrix printers, daisy-wheel printers, ink-jet printers, and laser printers.

Dot-Matrix Printers

A **dot-matrix printer** is an output device that uses tiny dots to create text and graphics on paper (see Figure 1.8). Just as graphics monitors use pixels to construct characters and pictures on a screen, dot-matrix printers similarly use dots of ink on pages of paper. Inside the dot-matrix printer a *printhead* is moved across the paper from left to right, and sometimes also from right to left (see Figure 1.8). This printhead may contain anywhere from 7 to 27 pins arranged in a vertical column. While most dot-matrix printers use 9 pins, more expensive printers with 18 or 24 pins are also fairly common. As the printhead moves horizontally, it

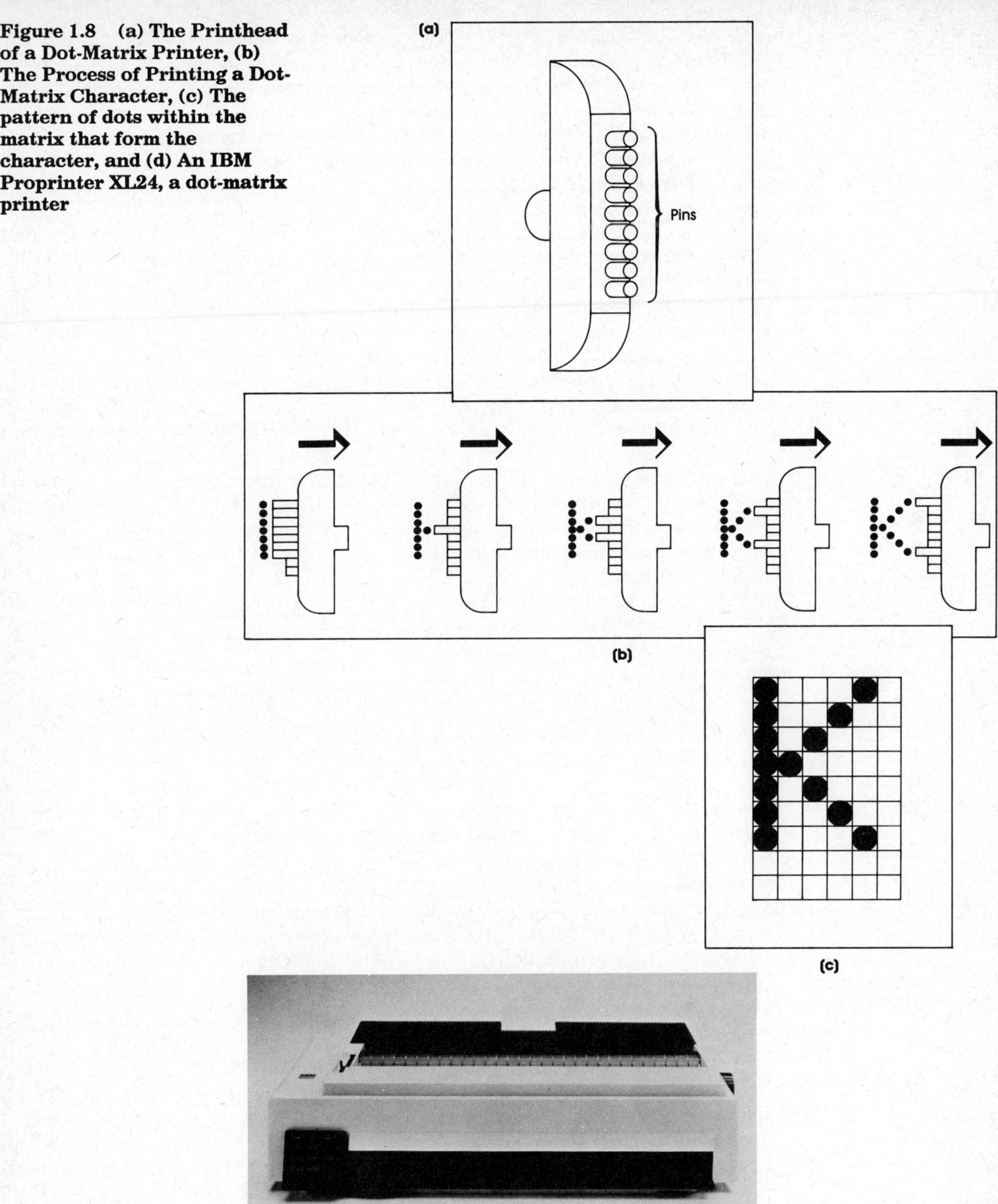

Figure 1.8 (a) The Printhead of a Dot-Matrix Printer, (b) The Process of Printing a Dot-Matrix Character, (c) The pattern of dots within the matrix that form the character, and (d) An IBM Proprinter XL24, a dot-matrix printer

constructs a character by repeatedly striking these pins against an inked ribbon and the paper. Electrical signals cause the appropriate pins to be thrust out at the proper moment to form the successive columns of dots that make up a character's image. Each column of the character is struck in turn against the ribbon and paper until the complete image has been formed. Dot-matrix printers are sometimes described as being impact printers because of the way the pins hit the ribbon and paper. This printing mechanism is most frequently used for text, but dot-matrix printers can usually produce graphics, too.

Dot-matrix printers are by far the most popular type of microcomputer printer. They are reasonably priced, fairly quick, and pretty reliable. Prices range between $150 and $3000, but the typical cost of an average 9-pin dot-matrix printer is about $500. The speed of a dot-matrix printer depends upon what print mode it is using. The fastest mode is called **draft mode**, in which characters are formed by just a single pass of the print head. Some expensive dot-matrix printers are able to achieve speeds of 400 characters per second in draft mode. Many dot-matrix printers also have a **near letter-quality (NLQ) mode**. In this mode, the printhead makes two or more passes over each character, slightly shifting its position each time. This tends to fill in the gaps between the dots and makes text appear more like it was produced by an electric typewriter. Using NLQ mode may slow some printers down to only 15 characters per second. Generating graphics with a dot-matrix printer can also be time consuming. Depending upon how dark the images are, it may take several minutes per page to produce graphics on a dot-matrix printer.

Daisy-Wheel Printers

A **daisy-wheel printer** uses a circular printing mechanism called a **daisy wheel**. Solid, raised characters are embossed on the ends of little "arms" arranged in a circle like the spokes of a wheel or the petals of a daisy. As this daisy wheel spins, a tiny, stationary hammer strikes the back of the proper character when it passes (see Figure 1.9). This impact drives the character pattern, which is embossed in reverse, against an inked ribbon and the paper. Daisy-wheel printers are true **letter-quality** printers because they produce well-defined text just like electric typewriters. Their prices are comparable with that of dot-matrix printers. Unlike dot-matrix printers, however, daisy-wheel printers cannot produce graphics. They are also noisier and slower than dot-matrix printers. The typical daisy-wheel printer can only print about 10 characters per second, and even the most expensive models generally cannot do better than 100 characters per second. Daisy-wheel printers are still fairly popular with microcomputer owners, but they are gradually being supplanted by 24-pin dot-matrix printers and laser printers.

Ink-Jet Printers

An **ink-jet printer** has a mechanism that squirts tiny, electrically-charged droplets of ink out of a nozzle and onto the paper (see Figure 1.10). (No pins or hammers strike the paper, so ink-jet printers are classified as nonimpact printers.) Ink-jet printers are fast, quiet, and can produce high-quality print, but they are slightly more expensive than dot-matrix printers. Some ink-jet printers have a tendency to clog their nozzle with ink and smear characters on paper. Many ink-jet printers, however, have the capability to print in color, a capability most other types of printers lack.

Figure 1.9 The Daisy-Wheel Printing Mechanism and a Daisy Wheel

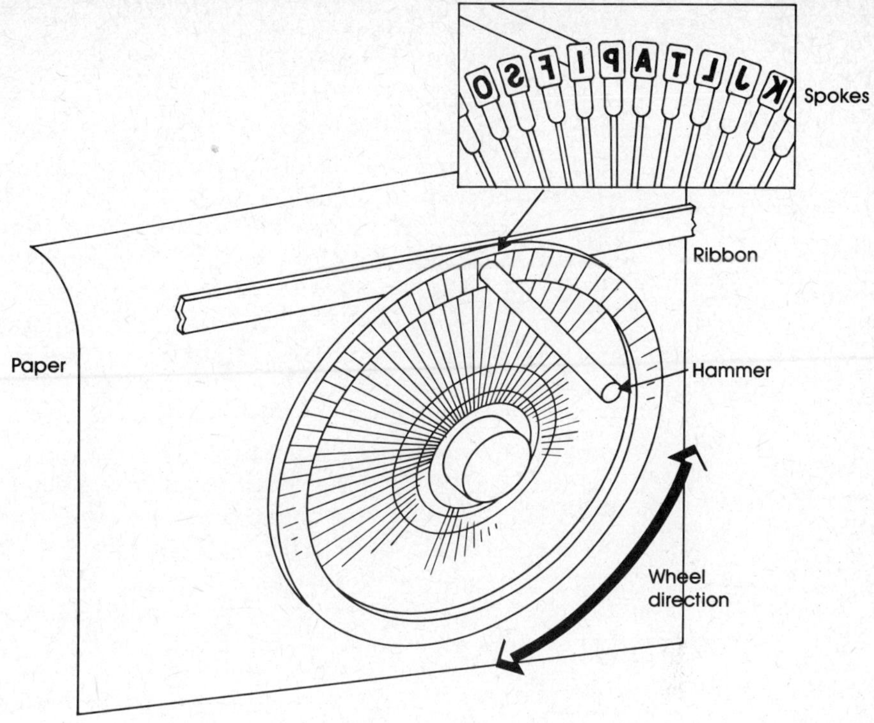

Figure 1.10 (above) Ink Jet Printing, and (below) The Hewlett-Packard PaintJet Color-Graphics Printer

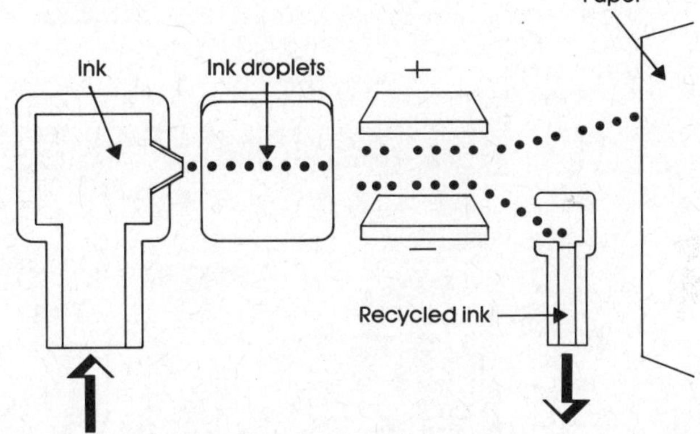

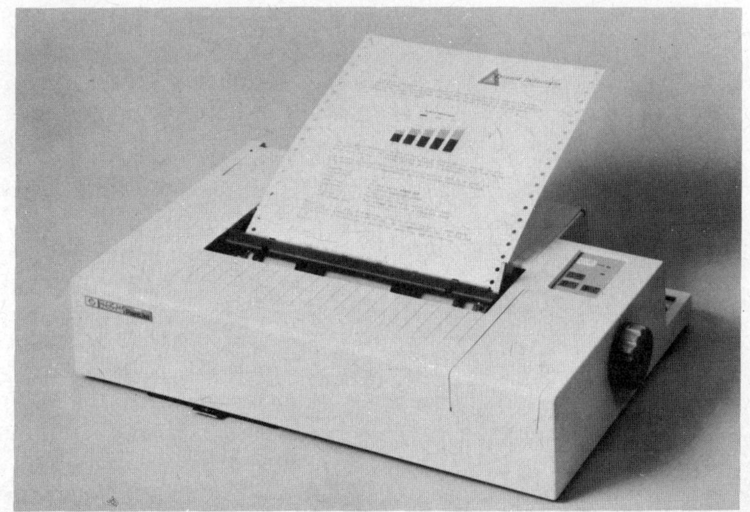

Laser Printers

A **laser printer** is an output device that uses tightly focused beams of light to transfer images to paper (see Figure 1.11). A tiny laser emits pulsating pinpoint bursts of light that are reflected off a special spinning mirror. This mirror reflects light onto a rotating drum. Light striking the drum causes it to become charged with electricity. An inklike toner is attracted to the drum in these electrically charged spots. When the drum is rolled over a piece of paper, the toner is transferred to the paper and an image is permanently fixed through a combination of heat and pressure. This image transfer process is similar to that found in a plain-paper photocopy machine. The result is high-quality text and graphics that almost look as if they were typeset. (Like ink-jet printers, laser printers are classified as nonimpact printers.)

Laser printers represent the most advanced printing technology. Although the images they produce are made up of dots, these dots are much smaller and more densely packed than the dots created with a dot-matrix printer. The typical microcomputer laser printer is capable of printing at a resolution of 300 dots per inch, both horizontally and vertically. This means 90,000 dots per square inch. Besides printing high-quality images, laser printers are also fast and quiet. The average speed of most laser printers is 8 pages per minute. This is equivalent to about 400 characters per second. Because laser printers don't use impact methods like dot-matrix and daisy-wheel printers, they are very quiet by comparison. The major disadvantage to laser printers is their cost. Prices generally start at around $1000. Despite the cost, more and more laser printers are being used with microcomputers every year. They are especially popular in office situations where the printer can be shared among several users.

Figure 1.11 The Hewlett-Packard LaserJet Series II Laser Printer

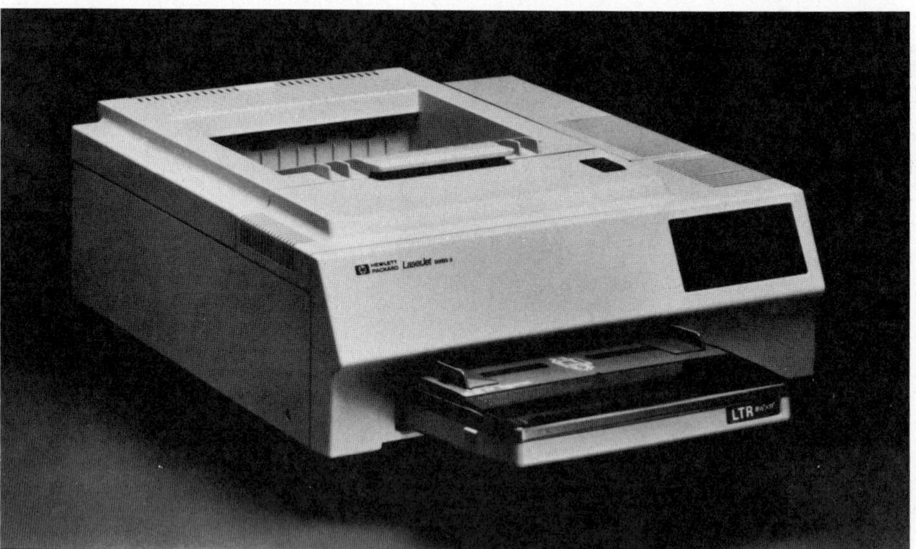

Software

By itself, computer hardware is useless. Programs are needed to operate the hardware. As we mentioned earlier, a program is simply a sequence of instructions that tells a computer what to do. **Software** is a general term that refers to any single program or group of programs. In contrast to hardware, which is constructed from physical materials like metal and plastic, software is built from knowledge, planning, and testing. A person who creates programs is called a **programmer**. Programmers use their knowledge of how a computer works to plan sets of instructions that accomplish useful tasks. These instructions are entered into the computer and repeatedly tested and modified until they achieve the desired results. As we said earlier, programs and data are generally kept on magnetic disks, where they can be accessed and used over and over again. Note that the disks themselves aren't the software, they're just the medium on which software is stored.

As an analogy, think of a stereo system. The amplifier, compact disc player, and speakers are the hardware. The amplifier is like the central processing unit and memory, the compact disc player is like a disk drive, and the speakers are like the display, except they present audio instead of video output. The music, which is stored on compact discs, is like software, which is stored on floppy disks. Just as you can amass a huge music collection by buying more compact discs, you can build a bigger software library by purchasing additional programs on floppy disks. The stereo system is of little use without the compact discs and the compact discs are useless without the stereo system. Similarly, a computer system is useless without software and software is useless without a computer system on which to run it.

Just as there are different types of hardware, there are also different types of software. Basically, there are three major categories: *system software*, *programming languages*, and *application software*.

System Software

System software handles the many details of managing a computer system. A computer's **operating system** makes up most of its system software. This is the set of programs that controls a computer's hardware and manages the use of software. One small part of the operating system, for example, is a program that identifies which key you've pressed, determines the character that corresponds to that key, and forms that character on the display screen. Another example is a program that lets you erase the contents of a magnetic disk. Some system software is built into a computer's ROM chips, while other system software comes on magnetic disk and must be purchased separately.

Programming Languages

Computer programs are developed with programming languages. A **programming language** is simply a set of symbols and rules to direct the operations of a computer. There are many different programming languages in common use, each designed to develop certain types of programs. A few of the most popular programming languages are BASIC, Pascal, C, FORTRAN, COBOL, and Ada. Although it can be helpful to learn a programming language for some very specific applications, most people who use computers don't actually program them. They just use programs, such as operating systems and application software, that have been developed by professional programmers.

Application Software

Application software is the software that applies the computer to useful tasks such as helping you create documents, figure your taxes, maintain mailing lists, and draw charts. Also called **application packages** or simply **applications**, these programs are the real reason most people buy and use microcomputers. The three most widely used applications follow.

- **Word Processing** A **word processing package** is software that helps you prepare documents by letting you enter, store, modify, format, copy, and print text.
- **Spreadsheet** A **spreadsheet package** is software that lets you manipulate tables of numbers, text, and formulas. It is an extremely flexible tool that can be used to handle typical accounting chores, monitor investments, balance a checkbook, and work out a budget.
- **Data Base Management** A **data base** is an organized collection of one or more files of related data. A file is a mass of individual data items kept together on a disk. A **data base management package** is software that lets you create, add to, delete from, update, rearrange, select from, print out, and otherwise administer data files such as mailing lists and inventories.

Besides these "big three" application packages, there are many other types of popular software, including the following:

- **Communications** Using an auxiliary device called a **modem**, a computer can transmit and receive programs and data over ordinary telephone lines. Communications software makes it possible for a computer to use a modem to call other computers and access on-line information services.
- **Graphics** Graphics packages let you use a computer to create all kinds of pictures including graphs, charts, maps, paintings, drawings, diagrams, blueprints, simulated slide shows, and animated presentations.
- **Desktop Publishing** Combining the results of word processing and graphics, desktop publishing or page layout software lets you use a computer and laser printer to produce near typeset quality documents.
- **Accounting** Accounting software lets you use a computer to record, analyze, and report business transactions.
- **Integrated Software** Integrated software combines word processing, spreadsheet, data base management, communications, and graphics applications in a single package.
- **Windowing Environment** Working closely with the operating system, a windowing environment allows you to divide your screen into a number of different boxes, or *windows*, and run a separate program in each one.
- **DOS Shell** A DOS shell is a program that enhances PC-DOS or MS-DOS, the operating system used with IBM and IBM-compatible microcomputers. Basically, it is an easy-to-use front-end to DOS that helps you execute commands and manage disk files.
- **Utilities** There are a host of small, specific programs called utilities that add handy features and functions to a particular operating system or application package. These include disk and file utilities, printer utilities, keyboard utilities, and desk accessories such as calculators, calendars, and address books.
- **On-Line References** Software to help you check your spelling, find a synonym, or look up a word's definition are all examples of on-line references.
- **Statistics and Math** Many programs exist for performing statistical analyses and helping solve mathematical equations.
- **Project Management** A project management package is software that helps you formally plan and control complex undertakings, such as the construction of a building, the development of a new product, or the installation of a large computer system.
- **Personal Finance and Taxes** Many programs exist for helping you manage your money and prepare your federal and state income tax returns.
- **Education** There is a wide range of programs for teaching skills and concepts, from learning the alphabet to designing physics experiments.

- **Entertainment** An amazing variety of microcomputer software exists for playing games, simulating cars and planes, and playing music.
- **Hypertext** A hypertext package is software that lets you store and retrieve all kinds of information in a nonsequential manner. In other words, you can randomly jump from topic to related topic, accessing any kind of information the computer can store, including text, graphics, audio, and video.
- **Expert System** An expert system is a computer program that contains a collection of facts and a list of rules for making inferences about those facts. Such software can use these facts and rules in a particular field to advise, analyze, categorize, diagnose, explain, identify, interpret, and teach.

Helpful Hints for Using a Microcomputer

Now that we've covered the general topics, let's go over a few specific details that can help prepare you for using a microcomputer.

Turning on the Computer

Sometimes, just turning on the computer can be an adventure. It seems that some manufacturers are fond of "hiding" the **power switch**. This has the practical purpose of making it difficult to turn off the computer by accident while in the middle of some critical task. Not being able to find the power switch, however, can make you feel lost before you even begin.

On the new IBM Personal System/2 computers, the power switch is a big red toggle right up front on the system unit. No problem here. On other computers, if the switch isn't immediately obvious up front, then it is probably on the right side of the system unit toward the rear. This is the case in IBM PCs, XTs, and ATs. Some models from other companies have the power switch mounted somewhere on the back side of the system unit or monitor.

Speaking of monitors, many color graphics displays have a separate power switch that must also be turned on, otherwise you will be looking at a permanently blank screen. The on/off switch is usually the top knob of three on the front of the monitor and is turned on by rotating it to the right. The other two knobs are the contrast and brightness controls, just like the ones on many television sets. If these three controls aren't right up front, they may be present as slightly protruding little disks located just under the bottom front edge of the monitor. Another possibility is the ever-popular back side of the monitor.

Operating the Printer

Like the system unit and monitor, the printer also has a power switch that must be turned on. This power switch is frequently positioned at the rear of the left or right side. In addition, there are at least three other buttons on most printers. Usually stationed on the top or front of the printer, these three buttons may be labeled On Line, Line Feed, and Form Feed. The **On Line** button is very important and is usually paired with an indicator light. When the On Line light is on, the printer is connected to and controlled by the computer, so that printing can occur. Make sure the On Line button is pressed so that the On Line light is on before attempting to print. The **Line Feed** and **Form Feed** buttons let you advance the paper in the printer, usually only when the printer is off line.

Caring for Floppy Disks

Although floppy disks are quite durable and can take quite a bit of punishment, there are a few guidelines you should follow in their handling:

1. Don't touch the exposed surfaces on 5¼-inch disks. Don't open the little metal door on 3½-inch disks.
2. Don't bend or fold 5¼-inch floppies.
3. Don't expose disks to extreme heat.
4. Keep 5¼-inch disks in their sleeves when not in use.
5. Don't write on 5¼-inch disks with pencils or hard point pens.
6. Keep your disks dry.
7. Don't expose disks to strong magnetic fields (keep them away from magnets and powerful motors).
8. Always try to keep at least one backup copy of all important disks.
9. Carefully insert and remove disks from disk drives. Wait until the drive's red access light is off before changing disks.

Conclusion

In this chapter of the *Software Guide*, you've learned what a microcomputer is, what it does, and what kinds of software are available. In addition, you've learned a few tips for turning on a microcomputer, operating a printer, and caring for floppy disks. This material sets the stage for the next chapter, in which you will complete lessons to teach you how to use PC-DOS and MS-DOS, the operating systems for IBM and IBM-compatible microcomputers.

Exercises

Multiple Choice

Choose the best selection to complete each statement.

_______ 1. A microcomputer is a computer in which the central processing unit consists of
   (a) a RAM chip. (c) a microprocessor chip.
   (b) a ROM chip. (d) a device controller chip.

_______ 2. A set of instructions that controls a computer's operation is
   (a) a program. (c) input.
   (b) data. (d) output.

_______ 3. The main circuit board of a computer is called the
   (a) expansion board. (c) bus.
   (b) device controller. (d) motherboard or system board.

_______ 4. IBM and IBM-compatible microcomputers use microprocessors from the
   (a) Motorola 68000 family. (c) Zilog Z80 family.
   (b) Intel 8088 family. (d) GTE G65SC816 family.

_______ 5. A byte is the amount of storage needed to hold a
   (a) single character. (c) single line.
   (b) single page. (d) single file.

_____ 6. Which of the following does NOT describe random access memory (RAM)?
- (a) It is temporary storage.
- (b) It loses its contents when the power is turned off.
- (c) It is permanently encoded at the factory.
- (d) It can be read and written over and over again.

_____ 7. The two most popular floppy disk sizes are
- (a) 3½-inch and 8-inch.
- (b) 5¼-inch and 8-inch.
- (c) 3½-inch and 5¼-inch.
- (d) 3-inch and 12-inch.

_____ 8. Which of the following types of display systems can present text and pictures on the screen, but in only a single color?
- (a) monochrome text display
- (b) monochrome graphics display
- (c) color graphics display
- (d) monochrome display adapter

_____ 9. Which of the following microcomputer keyboard keys is used to tell the computer to go ahead and process what was just typed?
- (a) Enter or Return key
- (b) Escape key
- (c) Control key
- (d) Function key

_____ 10. The most advanced and expensive type of printer in the following group is the
- (a) dot-matrix printer.
- (b) daisy-wheel printer.
- (c) ink-jet printer.
- (d) laser printer.

_____ 11. A set of programs that controls a computer's hardware and manages the use of software is called
- (a) an operating system.
- (b) a programming language.
- (c) an application package.
- (d) a data base management package.

_____ 12. Which of the following types of software lets you manipulate tables of numbers, text, and formulas?
- (a) word processing package
- (b) spreadsheet package
- (c) data base management package
- (d) operating system

_____ 13. Which of the following types of software lets you use a modem to transmit and receive programs and data over ordinary telephone lines?
- (a) communications package
- (b) graphics package
- (c) desktop publishing package
- (d) windowing package

_____ 14. Which of the following types of software lets you use a computer to record, analyze, and report business transactions?
- (a) graphics package
- (b) accounting package
- (c) DOS shell
- (d) utilities

_____ 15. Small, specific programs that add handy features and functions to a particular operating system or application package are called
- (a) on-line references.
- (b) hypertext programs.
- (c) spreadsheets.
- (d) utilities.

_____ 16. Which of the following types of software would be the best choice for maintaining a mailing list?
- (a) word processing package
- (b) spreadsheet package
- (c) data base management package
- (d) accounting package

_____ 17. Which of the following types of programs would you use to help plan and control the construction of a new office building?
- (a) word processing package
- (b) spreadsheet package
- (c) integrated software package
- (d) project management package

_____ 18. Which of the following types of software lets you store and retrieve all kinds of information in a nonsequential manner and then randomly jump from topic to related topic?
(a) word processing package
(b) spreadsheet package
(c) hypertext package
(d) expert system

_____ 19. Which printer button determines whether the printer is connected to and controlled by the computer?
(a) Power
(b) On Line
(c) Line Feed
(d) Form Feed

_____ 20. Which of the following should you NOT do to a floppy disk?
(a) Keep it in its sleeve when not in use.
(b) Keep it away from extreme heat.
(c) Keep it near a magnet when not in use.
(d) Keep it dry.

Fill-In

1. An __________ microcomputer works like a comparable IBM model and can run the same software.

2. At the lowest level, the basic operations of all computers can be summed up as input, __________, and output.

3. The __________ of a computer system is the electronic and mechanical equipment that make it work.

4. A microcomputer's motherboard contains the __________, which is a set of wires and connectors that link the CPU to memory and other computer components.

5. __________ is temporary storage for programs and data, which can be used and then overwritten by other programs and data. __________, on the other hand, is permanent storage encoded at the factory with frequently used programs and data that need never be changed.

6. Most microcomputers can be equipped with two basic types of disk drives: floppy disk drives and __________.

7. The number and size of a monitor's __________ determine its sharpness, or resolution.

8. The __________ is the display adapter that comes built onto the motherboards of high-end IBM Personal System/2 microcomputers.

9. Many microcomputers have an auxiliary input device known as a __________, which is a little box with one or more buttons that is glided across the table top.

10. On an IBM keyboard, the __________ Movement keys include Up Arrow, Down Arrow, Left Arrow, Right Arrow, Home, End, Page Up and Page Down.

11. __________ printers are by far the most popular type of microcomputer printer.

12. __________ is a general term that refers to any single program or group of programs.

13. BASIC, Pascal, C, FORTRAN, COBOL, and Ada are all examples of popular programming __________.

14. ____________________ software is the software that applies the computer to useful tasks such as helping you create documents, prepare a budget, or maintain a mailing list.

15. ____________________ packages let you use a computer to create all kinds of graphs, charts, maps, paintings, drawings, diagrams, slide shows, and presentations.

16. Combining the results of word processing and graphics software, ____________________ software lets you use a computer and laser printer to produce near typeset quality documents.

17. ____________________ software combines word processing, spreadsheet, data base management, communications, and graphics applications in a single package.

18. A ____________________ environment allows you to divide your screen into a number of different boxes and run a separate program in each one.

19. A ____________________ management package is software that helps you formally plan and control complex undertakings.

20. An ____________________ system is a computer program that contains a collection of facts and a list of rules for making inferences about those facts.

2

The PC-DOS Operating System

Learning Objectives

After reading this chapter, you should know how to do the following:

- Explain what a disk operating system is
- Explain why there are different versions of PC-DOS
- Boot PC-DOS with the computer turned off
- Boot PC-DOS with the computer turned on
- Obtain a directory listing of a disk's files
- Explain the structure of a PC-DOS file name
- Use the special PC-DOS keys
- Change the default disk drive
- Obtain a disk and memory status report
- Clear the display screen
- Format a diskette
- Format a system diskette
- Copy files
- Copy entire diskettes
- Change file names
- Erase files
- Display a text file on the screen
- Send a text file to the printer
- Run an application program
- Create and use DOS subdirectories
- Use DOS batch files

Introduction

An operating system is a set of programs that helps you use the hardware and software resources of a general-purpose computer. It's what you use to tell the computer to perform common tasks such as running application packages, managing disk storage, and controlling peripheral devices such as display screens and printers. In one sense, an operating system is like a toolbox that contains all kinds of utility programs to perform many of the little jobs that most users need. These utilities are like tools; some are used everyday by almost everyone, while others are more exotic and may only be used occasionally, even by experts.

A **disk operating system** (or **DOS**) is kept on a floppy or hard disk. When the computer system is turned on, some components of the operating system are loaded from disk into primary memory and remain there until the computer is shut off. These components, called **resident routines** or **internal commands**, are kept in memory because they are the most essential or the most frequently used parts of the operating system. The other components of a DOS are kept on disk and are temporarily loaded into memory only when they are needed or specifically requested. As a result, these latter commands are often called **transient routines** or **external commands**.

An important characteristic of a disk operating system is the abundance of utilities to deal with files that are stored on disks. A file, you'll recall, is just a collection of related data that is kept on a disk. Since most programs, text, and numerical data are kept in disk files, almost everything you do with computers involves working with files. Every computer user, therefore, must deal with an operating system to some extent. This chapter of the guide will teach you how to use the most popular disk operating system for IBM and IBM-compatible microcomputers.

PC-DOS and MS-DOS

PC-DOS, which stands for *Personal Computer Disk Operating System*, is by far the most popular operating system IBM offers for its microcomputers. It was written for IBM by Microsoft Corporation, which kept the right to also sell the same operating system itself under its own name, **MS-DOS**. Although there are some minor differences between PC-DOS and MS-DOS, from the average user's viewpoint they are virtually identical. The major distinction is that PC-DOS is generally used with IBM computers, and MS-DOS is used with the many compatible computers made by companies such as Compaq, AT&T, Tandy, and Zenith. From now on, everything we say about PC-DOS will also be true for MS-DOS, and so we'll just refer to both of them generically as DOS.

DOS Versions

Because computer technology changes so rapidly, an operating system like DOS is not a static entity. Operating systems must be constantly updated to accommodate new computer models and new capabilities for existing models. So far, there have been several official releases, or versions, of DOS. Although bugs have been worked out and improvements made over previous versions, the driving force behind each new release of DOS has been a new hardware capability, usually related to floppy or hard disk drives.

It's important to know which version of DOS you are using, because some hardware and software can only be used with more recent versions. Fortunately, each new version of DOS is **upwardly compatible** with former versions–that is, almost everything that worked with previous versions should work with the new version. So, you probably don't have to change the way you did things before unless you want to take advantage of the added capabilities of the new version. In fact, you usually don't have to buy the latest version of DOS each time a new release is issued. As long as the version you have works with your hardware and software, you can continue using it.

DOS versions are denoted by numbers such as 1.00, 2.10, and 3.30. The number to the left of the decimal point reflects a major classification; the numbers to the right represent more minor differences. The bigger the number, the more recent the version. Table 2.1 shows a summary of the DOS versions that have been released so far. Throughout this guide, we'll be using DOS 3.30 for all of our examples. Don't be concerned if you don't have the same version of DOS; everything we'll be covering will work for all versions 2.00 or newer.

Table 2.1

Version	Date	Hardware Support (Reason for New Version)
1.00	8/81	IBM PC single-sided floppy disk drive
1.10	5/82	IBM PC double-sided floppy disk drive
2.00	3/83	IBM XT 10 megabyte hard disk drive
2.10	10/83	IBM PCjr & Portable PC half-height floppy
3.00	8/84	IBM AT high-capacity floppy & hard disk
3.10	3/85	IBM AT network disks
3.20	12/85	IBM PC Convertible 3½-inch disk drive
3.30	3/87	IBM Personal System/2 disk drives
4.00	7/88	Hard disks larger than 35 megabytes

General Features of PC-DOS

PC-DOS provides many capabilities, both simple and complex. We'll be discussing some of its most used simple features, such as the following:

- **Booting Up with the Power Off** DOS can automatically load itself into memory when you turn the power on.
- **Booting Up with the Power On** DOS can be reloaded and reset without having to turn the power off and then on again.
- **Keeping Track of the Date and Time** Once you initially tell DOS the date and time, it will keep track of them until you turn the computer off or reboot.
- **Listing File Directories** You can instruct DOS to produce a directory of some or all of the files on a particular disk.
- **Using Special Keys** By pressing certain keys on the keyboard, you can tell DOS to cancel an input line, pause screen scrolling, cancel a command, print the screen, and echo input and output to the printer.
- **Changing the Default Drive** DOS lets you specify the disk drive it will assume when a drive designation isn't explicitly given.
- **Checking Disk and Memory Status** DOS can produce a report of useful information about a disk and primary memory.
- **Clearing the Screen** DOS lets you erase your display screen.
- **Formatting a Diskette** DOS lets you prepare a new diskette so that program and data files can be stored on it. It can also install itself on a new diskette if you tell it to do so.
- **Copying Files** DOS permits you to copy files onto the same disk or from one disk to another.
- **Copying Diskettes** DOS allows you to copy an entire diskette with a single command.
- **Changing File Names** DOS lets you choose new names for existing files.
- **Erasing Files** DOS allows you to delete unneeded files from a disk.
- **Displaying Text Files** You can have DOS display text files on your screen.
- **Printing Text Files** You can have DOS send text files to your printer.
- **Running Programs** You can tell DOS to run application programs such as VP-Expert.
- **Using Subdirectories** You can create, use, and remove subdirectories, which are like separate little disks on a large disk.
- **Using Batch Files** You can create and execute collections of DOS commands stored in special text files called batch files.

Getting Started

Although DOS is a rich and powerful microcomputer operating system, you can quite easily learn its most commonly used features. For the most part, these features are invoked by issuing commands to DOS. A **command** is simply a word or mnemonic (memory aid) abbreviation entered at the keyboard that tells DOS to run a particular program. Once DOS has been initially loaded into memory, it's constantly on the lookout for these commands. In the following lessons you'll learn most of the DOS commands you're likely to need. You'll also be introduced to general concepts about the keyboard, display, disks, and disk drives that you'll be using in this and later parts. Wherever it's useful, figures will actually show you what you should see on your computer screen at a given point. These screen views will help you as you go through each lesson's steps.

DOS 3.30 comes on two floppy disks; one is labeled DOS Startup and the other is entitled DOS Operating. Previous versions of DOS also came on two disks, but these were labeled DOS and DOS Supplemental Programs. If you are using one of these earlier versions of DOS, you just need the DOS disk. If you are using a computer with a hard disk or one connected to a local area network, DOS may already be installed on it, but you can still use the DOS floppy disk or disks for the following lessons.

As you go through the lessons, you will be given instructions on what to type. In this text we'll use **bold** print to indicate what you're supposed to type. It doesn't matter whether you use uppercase or lowercase. DOS ignores case when processing commands.

Lesson 1: Booting DOS

The first thing that you must do is turn on your computer and load DOS into primary memory. This process is often called *booting DOS*, *loading DOS*, or simply *starting DOS*.

Step 1: Insert the DOS Disk

With the computer shut off, grasp the DOS 3.30 Startup disk (or DOS disk for previous versions) by the label and remove it from the sleeve (be careful not to touch the exposed parts around the oval slot and circular hole if it is a 5¼-inch disk). Hold the disk with the label side up and the oval slot pointing toward the computer. If your computer uses 3½-inch disks, hold the disk with the label up and the metal door pointed toward the computer. Insert the disk into the A drive and close the disk drive door. If your computer has two disk drives, side by side, the A drive is the one on the left. If it has two half-height drives arranged vertically, the A drive is the one on the top. If there is only one floppy drive, then it is the A drive.

Step 2: Turn the Computer On

If you have a color display, turn it on by twisting the top knob on the front panel to the right. If you have a monochrome display, you don't need to turn it on because its power cord is plugged into the computer. Turn on the computer by flipping up the big red switch, which is located right up front on the system unit of IBM Personal System/2 computers, or at the rear of the right side of the system unit on older IBM models. You should hear the cooling fan begin to whir.

Step 3: Watch the Display and Wait

Once the power is turned on, the computer goes through some self-tests to ensure that it is working properly. One of these tests checks out all of the primary memory installed. This could take a few seconds or several minutes depending upon how much memory the computer has. So, if nothing appears to be happening for a couple of minutes, don't be alarmed. After the power-on self-tests are complete, the computer will access drive A to see if the DOS disk is there. You should see the little red access light go on and hear the disk drive whir and click. Assuming the computer is in working order, the disk drive door is properly closed, and there is nothing wrong with the DOS disk, the DOS command processor and internal commands will be loaded into main memory and a message such as the following will appear on your display screen:

```
Current date is Tue  1-01-1980
Enter new date (mm-dd-yy): _
```

Step 4: Enter the Date and Time

Type today's date in the form of mm-dd-yy or mm/dd/yy. In other words, type in the month number, a dash or slash, the day of the month, another dash or slash, and the last two digits of the year. Now press the **Enter** key. After you have entered the date, a message like this will appear:

```
Current time is  0:00:36.90
Enter new time: _
```

Type the hour, a colon, and the minute, then press the **Enter** key. If it's afternoon, add twelve to the hour as in the military fashion. For example, if it's 2 P.M., enter **14:00**. You can enter the second and the hundreds of seconds if you happen to carry a stopwatch and feel so inclined. However, just the hour and minute are sufficient. After you do this, your screen should look something like the screen in Figure 2.1. The A> on the last line is called the **DOS prompt**. It indicates that disk drive A is your default drive and that the DOS command processor is patiently waiting for you to enter a command. The **default drive** is the disk drive that DOS assumes you want to use unless you specify otherwise.

Note: Many computers now have a battery-maintained clock/calendar that makes entering the date and time unnecessary. If the current date and time presented by DOS are correct, all you have to do is press the Enter key each time in response.

Figure 2.1 Booting Up DOS

```
Current date is Wed  1-01-1980
Enter new date (mm-dd-yy): 7-13-89
Current time is  0:00:36.26
Enter new time: 7:51


The IBM Personal Computer DOS
Version 3.30 (C)Copyright International Business Machines Corp 1981, 1987
             (C)Copyright Microsoft Corp 1981, 1986

A>_
```

Lesson 2: Rebooting DOS

Occasionally, something goes wrong in a program and the computer may seem to be "stuck." Or, after working with a program you may have to "reinitialize" the computer, or bring it back to the way it was when you first turned it on. You could, of course, just shut the computer off and boot it up as we outlined in Lesson 1. There's another way, however, to reboot the computer without shutting it off.

Step 1: Press Ctrl-Alt-Del

DOS has a special combination of keypresses that will reboot the computer without having to shut it off first. All you have to do is press the keys marked **Ctrl**, **Alt**, and **Del**, and hold them down at the same time for a moment.

Step 2: Watch the Display and Wait

In most cases, the screen will go blank, the computer will beep, and the disk drive will spin and blink its red access light just like it did when you first turned it on. If all this doesn't happen, a serious program error has probably overwritten a crucial part of DOS in memory and you will have to shut the computer off and boot it up as you did in Lesson 1. If all is well, DOS will again ask you to supply the date and time.

Step 3: Enter the Date and Time

After you enter the date and time as you did in Lesson 1, DOS will once again display its copyright message and the system prompt, as shown in Figure 2.1.

Lesson 3: Listing a Disk File Directory

As we mentioned before, programs, data, and text are kept on disks in files. Every file has a name, size, creation date, and creation time associated with it. DOS can display this information for you if you use the directory command.

Step 1: Enter the Directory Command

At the DOS prompt, type in the letters **dir** and press the **Enter** key. As with all DOS commands, it doesn't matter if you use uppercase or lowercase letters. DIR is is the abbreviation for the DOS directory command that will list the directory of the default disk on your display screen. Remember that the default disk is the one in the disk drive that DOS assumes you are currently working on, and its letter is indicated by the DOS prompt. Right now, your default disk drive should be A, so the DIR command will list the file names, sizes, and creation dates and times for all the files on the floppy disk in drive A. Figure 2.2 shows what the screen looks like when it stops scrolling.

Figure 2.2 Listing a Directory

```
COMMAND  COM    25307   3-17-87  12:00p
ANSI     SYS     1678   3-17-87  12:00p
COUNTRY  SYS    11285   3-17-87  12:00p
DISPLAY  SYS    11290   3-17-87  12:00p
DRIVER   SYS     1196   3-17-87  12:00p
FASTOPEN EXE     3919   3-17-87  12:00p
FDISK    COM    48216   3-18-87  12:00p
FORMAT   COM    11616   3-18-87  12:00p
KEYB     COM     9056   3-17-87  12:00p
KEYBOARD SYS    19766   3-17-87  12:00p
MODE     COM    15487   3-17-87  12:00p
NLSFUNC  EXE     3060   3-17-87  12:00p
PRINTER  SYS    13590   3-17-87  12:00p
REPLACE  EXE    11775   3-17-87  12:00p
SELECT   COM     4163   3-17-87  12:00p
SYS      COM     4766   3-17-87  12:00p
VDISK    SYS     3455   3-17-87  12:00p
XCOPY    EXE    11247   3-17-87  12:00p
EGA      CPI    49065   3-18-87  12:00p
LCD      CPI    10752   3-17-87  12:00p
4201     CPI    17089   3-18-87  12:00p
5202     CPI      459   3-17-87  12:00p
       22 File(s)     9216 bytes free

A>_
```

This is the directory of the PC-DOS 3.30 DOS Startup floppy disk. (If you are using a different version of DOS, the directory will be somewhat different.) Listed are the names, sizes, and creation dates and times of all the files on the DOS Startup disk. Notice that each file's name has two parts: a **primary file name**, which can be up to eight characters long, and a three-letter **extension**. We'll have more to say about this file name format later in this lesson. The number to the immediate right of each file's name is its size in bytes. A byte, you'll recall, is the amount of storage needed to hold a single character. Finally, listed with each file is the date and time it was created or last changed. So, for example, the file FORMAT.COM is made up of 11,616 bytes and was created at 12:00 P.M. on March 18, 1987.

At the very bottom of the listing, DOS informs you that there are 22 files in the directory and 9,216 bytes of empty room left on the disk. As you can imagine, it's pretty important to be able to see what's on a disk and how much room is left. For this reason, DIR is one of most frequently used DOS commands.

Incidentally, most of the files that you see in this directory listing with an extension of COM or EXE are external commands or transient routines of DOS. These are programs that reside on the DOS disk until you specifically call them up. In contrast, the DIR command is an internal command or resident routine. It too is a component program of DOS, but because it's used so frequently it's loaded into memory when DOS is booted and it's kept there. This means that DIR is not stored by itself in a separate file on the DOS disk; once you've booted up, you don't need the DOS disk in drive A to use the directory command.

Step 2: Examine Another Disk's Directory

The DIR command can also be used to list the directory of a disk in a drive other than the current default drive. You can do this by specifying the disk drive designation after typing dir. For example, to list the directory of a disk in drive B, you could enter this command:

dir b:

The **b:** is the designation for the B disk drive. If you have a computer with two floppy drives, remove the DOS disk from drive A, insert it into drive B, close the door, and enter **dir b:**. You should see the same directory listing you saw in Step 1 of this lesson. After you're done looking at the directory of drive B, make sure to put the DOS disk back into drive A.

If your computer has a hard disk drive and no second floppy drive, try entering **dir c:**. You should see some kind of directory listing, though it will probably be different from the one in Figure 2.2. This difference exists because many additional files are most likely stored on your hard disk. Note that the hard disk is usually referred to as the C drive regardless of whether a B floppy drive is installed.

Step 3: Look For a Specific File

Frequently, you'd like to be able to check if a particular file is on a disk without having to look at the entire directory. The DIR command can do this for you if you give it the name of the file you're looking for. All you have to do is enter the name of the file after typing dir. Then DOS either lists an abbreviated directory with only that file in it or tells you the file is not there. For example, enter this command:

dir a:format.com

Figure 2.3 shows what you should see on your screen.

DOS File Names This is a good time to digress a bit and discuss DOS file names in more detail. First of all, notice that each file in the directory you listed has a unique name. No two files in the same directory can have the same name because DOS wouldn't be able to tell them apart. Two files on different disks, however, can have the same name. As we mentioned before, a file's full name can consist of

Figure 2.3 Looking for a Specific File

```
A>dir a:format.com

 Volume in drive A has no label
 Directory of  A:\

FORMAT   COM    11616   3-18-87  12:00p
        1 File(s)      9216 bytes free

A>_
```

two parts: a primary filename and an optional extension. The first part, or **file name** as IBM calls it, can be from one to eight characters long. It can include any of the characters you see on the keyboard except for the following, which are considered invalid in file names:

. " / \ [ ] : | < > + = ; ,

The second part, an optional short name, is called an **extension**. It is separated from the primary filename by a period and has from one to three characters in it. These characters also can be any of the keyboard characters except those invalid ones we just listed. If a file's name does have an extension, you must use both parts when telling DOS to do something with that file. Extensions are most often used to further classify files. For example, here are some of the more common file name extensions along with the types of files they usually designate:

.COM DOS external command files and other programs
.EXE Executable program files
.SYS DOS system configuration and device driver files
.BAT DOS batch files
.BAS BASIC language source code files
.PAS Pascal language source code files
.FOR FORTRAN language source code files
.ASM Assembly language source code files
.TXT Ordinary text files
.ASC ASCII files
.DOC Document files for some word processing programs
.WKS Lotus 1-2-3 Release 1A worksheet files
.WK1 Lotus 1-2-3 Release 2 and 2.01 worksheet files
.DBF dBASE III PLUS data base files

Finally, a file name can be prefaced with the designation of the disk drive that it's on. For example, A:FORMAT.COM is the specification for the file containing the FORMAT command on the DOS disk in drive A. Note that the colon must be used to separate the disk drive letter from the filename.

Step 4: Look for a Specific Group of Files

Not only can the DIR command find a single file on a disk, it can also be used to list a group of files if their names have some characters in common. This is possible through the use of the DOS global filename characters, * and ?. These characters can be included in a filename or extension to give you greater flexibility in designating DOS files. The * character can be used in a file specification to symbolize any character or group of characters. For example, *.SYS means "any file with an extension of SYS." The ? character is used to symbolize any single character. For example, MO?E.COM means "any file that has an extension of COM and a four-letter filename beginning with MO and ending with an E." Both global file name characters can be used together in the same specification, too. For example, ????.* means "any file with at most four characters in its first part." Try these examples yourself:

dir *.sys
dir mo?e.com
dir ????.*

Figure 2.4 shows what you should see on your screen after entering the command **dir *.sys.**

Figure 2.4 Looking for a Group of Files

```
A>dir *.sys

 Volume in drive A has no label
 Directory of  A:\

ANSI     SYS     1678   3-17-87  12:00p
COUNTRY  SYS    11285   3-17-87  12:00p
DISPLAY  SYS    11290   3-17-87  12:00p
DRIVER   SYS     1196   3-17-87  12:00p
KEYBOARD SYS    19766   3-17-87  12:00p
PRINTER  SYS    13590   3-17-87  12:00p
VDISK    SYS     3455   3-17-87  12:00p
        7 File(s)     9216 bytes free

A>_
```

Lesson 4: Using Special DOS Keys

Like most software, DOS assigns special meanings to certain keys and combinations of keypresses. You've already learned some of these. For example, you know that you must press the Enter key after typing in a command. This tells DOS to go ahead and process that command. The Backspace key can be used to correct typing errors on a line before the Enter key has been pressed. Finally, you learned in Lesson 2 that pressing the Control (Ctrl), Alternate (Alt), and Delete (Del) keys all at the same time will reboot DOS without having to shut off and then turn the power back on. Let's explore some of the other keys DOS uses.

Step 1: Press the Escape Key to Cancel a Line

As you've probably already discovered, it's pretty easy to make typing mistakes when using a keyboard. If the command you're typing is short, and you haven't pressed the Enter key yet, the easiest way to fix a mistake is to backspace over it and retype it. If the command is long, or if you really messed up, you can cancel the entire line you just typed and start all over again. To do this, just press the Escape (Esc) key. For example, type the following line at the DOS prompt (but don't press the Enter key):

This line is really messed up!

Let's say what you really meant to type in was **dir**, and you realized your mistake before you pressed the Enter key. Just press **Escape** to cancel this line. When you do this, DOS will display a / (slash) after the exclamation point to signal that this line has been canceled and it will skip down to the next line so you can start over again. Enter **dir** and you'll see the familiar DOS directory again.

Lesson 5: Changing the Default Disk Drive

So far, you've been doing all your work on the A disk drive. The DOS prompt has been A>, which indicates that drive A is your current default disk drive. Thus, whenever you enter a command that doesn't explicitly specify a particular disk drive, the A drive is assumed. For example, when you enter **dir**, you get a directory of the disk in the default drive, which is currently drive A. If your computer has more than one disk drive, and most IBMs and IBM-compatibles do, you may sometime want to change your default drive from A to B, or to C if you have a hard disk. DOS makes it easy to take advantage of this feature, which is also called *switching drives*.

Step 1: Enter the Designation of the New Default Drive

If you have a computer with two floppy drives, you can change your default drive from A to B by typing **b:** and pressing the **Enter** key. If you have a computer with a hard disk, you can change your default drive from A to the hard disk by typing **c:** and pressing the **Enter** key. As soon as you do this, DOS responds with a new prompt, which indicates the new default drive. So, if you have two floppy drives and you enter **b:**, DOS responds with B> as the new prompt. If you have a hard disk and you enter **c:**, DOS responds with C> as the new prompt.

Step 2: Use the New Default Drive

If you have two floppy drives, remove the DOS disk from drive A and put it into the B drive and close the door. Now enter a DIR command, such as **dir *.sys.** The directory listing you get now will be of the new default drive, B or C (see Figure 2.7). Although this might not seem terribly exciting at the moment, being able to change the default drive easily enables you to make full use of all of your installed disk drives. As you become more proficient with DOS and application packages, you'll find yourself switching default disk drives often. For example, on systems with two floppy drives, you may leave the DOS disk in drive A and a disk containing a particular application program in drive B. Then, after booting up, you would switch to drive B to run your application program.

Figure 2.7 Changing the Default Disk Drive

```
A>b:

B>dir *.sys

 Volume in drive B has no label
 Directory of  B:\

ANSI     SYS     1678   3-17-87  12:00p
COUNTRY  SYS    11285   3-17-87  12:00p
DISPLAY  SYS    11290   3-17-87  12:00p
DRIVER   SYS     1196   3-17-87  12:00p
KEYBOARD SYS    19766   3-17-87  12:00p
PRINTER  SYS    13590   3-17-87  12:00p
VDISK    SYS     3455   3-17-87  12:00p
        7 File(s)      9216 bytes free

B>a:

A>_
```

Step 3: Switch Back to Disk Drive A

Enter **a:** to change the default directory back to the A drive. If you put the DOS disk in drive B, remove it and put it back into the A drive.

Lesson 6: Checking Disk and Memory Status

You've already learned how to use the DIR command to examine the contents of a disk's directory. In addition to this, DOS provides a command that can display a status report about a disk and the memory installed in your computer. This report contains some interesting and useful information. With DOS 3.30, this command is on the DOS Operating disk. If you're using DOS 3.30, take the DOS Startup disk out of drive A and replace it with the DOS Operating disk. If you're using a previous version of DOS, you don't need to change disks.

Step 1: Enter CHKDSK

With the appropriate disk in drive A, type **chkdsk** and press the **Enter** key. This will invoke the DOS check disk command and produces a report on your screen that looks something like the Figure 2.8. If you're not using DOS version 3.30 or if your computer has more or less than 512 kilobytes (512K) of primary memory, the numbers in your report will be different.

Step 2: Examine the Status Report

This status report tells you several useful things. It tells you that the total capacity of the disk currently in the default drive is 362,496 bytes (equivalent to about 100 pages of text). Admittedly, the "0 bytes in 1 hidden files" statement doesn't make much sense. You can simply ignore it in this case. The hidden files mentioned in the report are parts of DOS that are kept on the disk, but do not appear in the disk

Figure 2.8 The CHKDSK Report

```
A>chkdsk

   362496 bytes total disk space
    53248 bytes in 3 hidden files
   300032 bytes in 22 user files
     9216 bytes available on disk

   524288 bytes total memory
   399984 bytes free

A>_
```

directory. These files contain important DOS programs that are kept hidden from you so that you don't rename, change, or delete them. The CHKDSK report then tells you that there are 31 ordinary user files on the disk and that they occupy 307,200 bytes of space. That leaves 55,296 bytes of empty space still on the disk. Finally, CHKDSK tells you that 524,288 bytes (or 512K) of primary memory are installed in this computer and that 472,064 bytes of these are free for use by application programs. The difference between these latter two figures, 52,224 bytes, is the amount of primary memory taken up by the parts of DOS that remain resident–the command processor and the internal commands.

Lesson 7: Clearing the Screen

By now, you've probably accumulated quite a collection of commands and directory listings on your screen. Although this does no harm, it can be a bit distracting. Or, perhaps you want to type a sequence of commands and then do a print screen, and you would like to start off with a clean slate. Don't worry, it's easy to tell DOS to erase the screen.

Step 1: Enter CLS

To clear the screen, simply type **cls** and press the **Enter** key. DOS will then erase everything from the screen and start you off again with the system prompt on the first line in the upper left corner.

Lesson 8: Formatting a Diskette

Before a new floppy disk can be used to store programs and data files, it must undergo an initial preparation known as formatting. This preparation is not done at the factory, so you must do it with your own computer for each brand new diskette you're going to use. Although you usually format a new diskette only once, you can format a previously formatted disk in order to clear it off completely. Formatting a floppy basically consists of the following procedures:

- Checking the diskette for bad spots
- Wiping out any information that might be on the diskette
- Building a directory that will hold information about the files that will be on the diskette
- Marking off the empty space into equal-sized chunks called **sectors**
- Copying DOS onto the diskette if specified to do so

The DOS FORMAT command can automatically do all this for you.

Step 1: Get a Floppy Disk to Format

For this lesson you'll need a new floppy disk or a previously used disk that can be completely erased. If you are going to format a diskette that's not new, double check to make sure it doesn't have any programs or data files on it that you want to keep. Formatting a disk erases everything that's on it.

If it is a used 5¼-inch diskette, also make sure that it doesn't have a write-protect tab on it. If you hold the diskette right side up with your thumb on the label, you should be able to see a little square notch cut into it on the left edge. If this notch is not covered up, then it's not write-protected and it's all right to use. If the diskette has a gummed tab covering the notch, then remove the tab. If the diskette has no notch, then it's permanently write-protected and you'll have to use another diskette.

Step 2: Put the DOS Startup Disk in A and the New Disk in B

On a computer with two floppy disk drives, make sure the DOS Startup disk is in drive A. Put the disk you want to format into drive B and close both doors. If your computer has only one floppy disk drive, just make sure the DOS Startup disk is in it. The FORMAT command will tell you when to put the new diskette in.

Step 3: Enter the FORMAT Command

On a computer with two floppy disk drives, type **format b:** and press the **Enter** key. On a computer with just one floppy drive, type **format a:** and press the **Enter** key. The FORMAT command will then tell you to insert the new diskette into drive B (for two-floppy systems) or drive A (for single-floppy systems). Insert the disk as indicated, and press the **Enter** key.

Step 4: Wait for FORMAT to Finish

The formatting procedure will take a minute or so, during which you should see the disk drive access light go on. When the procedure is done, the FORMAT command will tell you how much room is on the disk and if it contained any bad sectors. The command will then ask you if you want to format another diskette and you can enter **n** for no. You'll then get the DOS prompt back again. When you're done, your screen should look something Figure 2.9.

Figure 2.9 shows you that there are 362,496 bytes of total disk space and all of that space is available for files. In other words, no bad areas were detected. If there were any bad sectors found on the disk, less space would be available. DOS would mark these sectors as unusable and prevent them from being used to store files.

Figure 2.9 Formatting a Diskette

```
A>format b:
Insert new diskette for drive B:
and strike ENTER when ready

Format complete

     362496 bytes total disk space
     362496 bytes available on disk

Format another (Y/N)?n
A>_
```

Lesson 9: Formatting a System Diskette

The diskette you've just formatted can now be used to store programs and data files. It cannot, however, be used to boot the computer because it does not have DOS installed on it. If you want to format a diskette so that DOS is installed, the procedure is slightly different.

Step 1: Use the /S Parameter

Many DOS commands can be given options that specify a slightly different way of performing their tasks. The FORMAT command, for example, can be instructed to install the operating system on the disk it's preparing. To do this, simply type /s after the drive designator of the disk to format. The /s tells FORMAT to put the DOS internal commands and the command processor on the disk being formatted. You can try this out by reformatting the disk you just formatted as we outlined in Lesson 8. This time, however, enter this command:

format b:/s

Step 2: Examine the Disk's Directory

Now the FORMAT command will tell you that the system was transferred and that 78,848 bytes were used by the operating system. Only 283,648 bytes are left available on the disk. Enter **dir b:**. Your screen should look like Figure 2.10. Notice that only the file COMMAND.COM is on the new system disk. It does not contain any of the external command files that are on the DOS disk. So, although you could boot up with this new disk, and you could execute internal commands such as DIR, you could not use any external commands such as CHKDSK or FORMAT unless you somehow copied their command files onto it.

Figure 2.10 Formatting a System Diskette

```
A>format b:/s
Insert new diskette for drive B:
and strike ENTER when ready

Format complete
System transferred

    362496 bytes total disk space
     78848 bytes used by system
    283648 bytes available on disk

Format another (Y/N)?n
A>dir b:

 Volume in drive B has no label
 Directory of  B:\

COMMAND  COM    25307   3-17-87  12:00p
        1 File(s)    283648 bytes free

A>_
```

Lesson 10: Copying Files

Once a diskette has been formatted, it can be used to store program and data files. But how do you get files onto the new diskette? One way is by using the DOS COPY command. The COPY command can be used to duplicate one or more files on the same or on different diskettes. As a very versatile command, COPY can be used in several different ways.

Step 1: Copy a Single File (the Long Way)

Let's use the COPY command to copy a single file from the DOS Startup disk onto your newly formatted disk. For starters, we'll do it the longhand way and then we'll show you the shortcut. To copy the file FORMAT.COM from the DOS Startup disk onto your new disk, first make sure the DOS Startup disk is in drive A and the new disk is in drive B. Then enter this command:

copy a:format.com b:format.com

The first file name is the *source*, or what you're copying from–the file FORMAT.COM on the disk in drive A. The second file name is the *target*, or what you're copying to–a file named FORMAT.COM on the disk in drive B. After you do this, DOS will tell you that one file was copied. If you enter **dir b:** you should see the file FORMAT.COM in the directory of the disk in drive B. Figure 2.11 shows what you should see on your screen.

Figure 2.11 Copy a File

```
A>copy a:format.com b:format.com
        1 File(s) copied

A>dir b:

 Volume in drive B has no label
 Directory of  B:\

COMMAND  COM    25307   3-17-87  12:00p
FORMAT   COM    11616   3-18-87  12:00p
        2 File(s)    271360 bytes free

A>_
```

Step 2: Copy a Single File (the Short Way)

In most cases, if you omit certain information, DOS will assume the default values. For example, if you don't supply a disk drive designation in front of a filename, DOS will assume that you mean the default drive. Similarly, if you don't specify a name for the target file, the COPY command will assume that it is to use the same name as the source. This assumption will work as long as the source and the target files are on different disks. So, another way to copy FORMAT.COM would be to enter this command:

copy format.com b:

This command means copy the file FORMAT.COM on the disk in the default drive to the disk in drive B and give it the same name. Try this shorter command. Realize, however, that you will be copying the FORMAT.COM on drive A to the FORMAT.COM that already exists on drive B from our first copy operation. If you choose a name that already exists as the target, DOS will happily copy over it, destroying whatever was in that file before. Since we're copying the exact same file, there's no problem here. As a rule, however, you should be very careful about the name you choose for a target file. If it already exists on the disk you're copying to, the original version will be overwritten.

Step 3: Copy a Group of Files

By using the global file name characters * and ? we introduced in Lesson 3, you can copy several files all at once with a single COPY command. For example, with the DOS Startup disk in drive A and your newly formatted disk in drive B, enter this command:

copy *.* b:

This will copy every single file on the disk in the default drive to the disk in drive B. Figure 2.12 shows what your screen should look like when this command is completed.

Step 4: Copy a File to the Same Disk

All the examples we've covered so far have copied files from one disk to another. Also, the target file names have all been the same as the source file names. This arrangement, however, needn't always be so. The COPY command can be used to duplicate a file on the same disk. The only catch is that you have to choose a different name for the target. Remember that no two files in the same directory can have the same name.

Figure 2.12 Copying a Group of Files

```
COMMAND.COM
ANSI.SYS
COUNTRY.SYS
DISPLAY.SYS
DRIVER.SYS
FASTOPEN.EXE
FDISK.COM
FORMAT.COM
KEYB.COM
KEYBOARD.SYS
MODE.COM
NLSFUNC.EXE
PRINTER.SYS
REPLACE.EXE
SELECT.COM
SYS.COM
VDISK.SYS
XCOPY.EXE
EGA.CPI
LCD.CPI
4201.CPI
5202.CPI
        22 File(s) copied

A>_
```

One common reason for duplicating a file on the same disk with a different name is for backup purposes. Let's say that you are going to change an existing file. If that file is especially important, you might want to keep a copy of the original version before you change it. One of the great advantages of using computers is the ease with which they can copy files. So, before you change your file, make a copy of it and give the copy a different name. As an example, with your DOS disk in drive A and your newly formatted disk in drive B, enter this command:

copy b:format.com b:format.bak

This will create a copy of the FORMAT.COM file on the disk in drive B and it will be named FORMAT.BAK (BAK for backup). Now you can go ahead and make your modifications, safe in the knowledge that you've retained a copy of the original file.

Lesson 11: Copying an Entire Diskette

DOS has a more specific copy command that lets you copy an entire diskette all at once. What's more, this command automatically formats the target diskette if it's new. When you need an exact copy of an entire diskette, the DISKCOPY command can do the trick. DISKCOPY only works, however, if the source and target are the same type of disk. For instance, you cannot use the DISKCOPY command to duplicate the contents of a 5¼-inch diskette on a 3½-inch diskette. To see how the DISKCOPY command does work, let's make an exact copy of our DOS Startup diskette on the new diskette we've been working with.

Step 1: Put the DOS Operating Disk in Drive A

With DOS 3.30, DISKCOPY is an external command stored on the DOS Operating disk. So, the first step is to put the DOS Operating disk into drive A.

Step 2: Issue the DISKCOPY Command

If your computer has two identical floppy disk drives, enter this command:

diskcopy a: b:

If your computer has only one floppy drive or two drives that are of different types, such as a 5¼-inch drive and a 3½-inch drive, enter this command instead:

diskcopy a: a:

Step 3: Follow the Directions

The DISKCOPY command will tell you which drive to put your source and target diskettes into and when to do so. Remember: the DOS Startup diskette is the source, and the new diskette is the target. If your machine has only one floppy drive, you may have to swap the source and target diskettes in drive A several times. When it's done, DISKCOPY will ask you if you want to copy another diskette and you can enter **n** for no. If you have two floppy drives, Figure 2.13 shows what you should see on your screen when DISKCOPY is done.

Figure 2.13 Copying an Entire Diskette

```
A>diskcopy a: b:

Insert SOURCE diskette in drive A:

Insert TARGET diskette in drive B:

Press any key when ready . . .

Copying 40 tracks
9 Sectors/Track, 2 Side(s)


Copy another diskette (Y/N)?n


A>_
```

DISKCOPY is a very useful command for making backup copies of especially important diskettes. In fact, the documentation that comes with many software packages suggests that you use the DISKCOPY command to duplicate all of your original diskettes as soon as you get them. Furthermore, they say that you should put the originals away for safekeeping and only use your copies. Then, if you should accidentally erase something or if a diskette you use daily should become damaged or wear out, you would still have your original diskettes from which to make additional copies. These are good suggestions, and DISKCOPY will work fine as long as your software is not copy-protected.

Lesson 12: Changing File Names

When a file is originally created, the name it's given isn't set in stone; DOS lets you change file names very easily. Perhaps you've thought up a more appropriate name, or you want to abbreviate a long name. Another reason to change a file name is that you want to copy a file onto a disk that already has a file of the same name. If you don't change the name of the file already on the disk, copying a new file of the same name onto the disk will destroy the original file's contents. The DOS RENAME command allows you to change the names of one or more files.

Step 1: Rename a Single File

Changing a single file's name is quite easy. Just type rename (or its abbreviation, ren), followed by the file name you want to change, and then the new name that file is to have. For example, put the copy of the DOS Startup disk you made in Lesson 11 in drive A and enter this command:

rename format.com format.bak

Now enter this command to see what you've done:

dir format.*

Your screen should look like Figure 2.14. The directory shows that you've successfully changed the name of FORMAT.COM to FORMAT.BAK. This procedure would be very useful if you wanted to copy a new version of the FORMAT.COM file to your disk, yet still keep a copy of the original version. Since the backup version is safely stored as FORMAT.BAK, you could now copy a new FORMAT.COM onto your disk.

Figure 2.14 Renaming a File

```
A>rename format.com format.bak

A>dir format.*

 Volume in drive A has no label
 Directory of  A:\

FORMAT   BAK     11616   3-18-87  12:00p
        1 File(s)      9216 bytes free

A>_
```

Before you go on, change FORMAT.BAK back to FORMAT.COM so that the DOS Startup disk copy is like it was before. This time, however, try using the abbreviated form of the RENAME command:

ren format.bak format.com

Step 2: Rename Several Files at Once

By using the global file name characters * and ?, you can rename several files at once. For example, with a single command you could rename each file on your DOS Startup disk copy with an extension of EXE, and give it an extension of BAK. Try entering this command:

ren *.exe *.bak

Now enter this directory command to see what you've done:

dir *.bak

Your screen should look like Figure 2.15. There are now no files on your disk with EXE extensions. They all have BAK extensions instead. Before you go on, change them all back to the way they were with this command:

ren *.bak *.exe

Figure 2.15 Renaming a Group of Files

```
A>ren *.exe *.bak

A>dir *.bak

 Volume in drive A has no label
 Directory of  A:\

FASTOPEN BAK     3919   3-17-87  12:00p
NLSFUNC  BAK     3060   3-17-87  12:00p
REPLACE  BAK    11775   3-17-87  12:00p
XCOPY    BAK    11247   3-17-87  12:00p
        4 File(s)     9216 bytes free

A>_
```

Lesson 13: Erasing Files

Just as you accumulate old memos, notes, letters, and other scraps of this or that on your desk, disks can also become cluttered with unneeded files. Occasionally, it's necessary to clean up a bit and discard those items that you know you no longer need. Once you throw something away, however, it may be difficult or even impossible to get it back again. Be careful, therefore, to discard only files you're sure you can't use anymore. DOS makes it very easy to erase files, but it has no provision to unerase, or restore, them. Use the DOS ERASE command with caution.

Step 1: Erase a Single File

To erase a single file, just type in **erase** or **del** (for delete) and follow it with the name of the file you want to erase. Put your DOS Startup disk copy in drive A. Because it is a copy and you know that everything on it is also on the original DOS Startup disk, you can safely erase files. Nevertheless, we want to emphasize caution again. Data and programs are most frequently lost as the result of an accidentally or carelessly entered ERASE command than from any other cause. The original 5¼-inch disks that come with PC-DOS when you purchase it from IBM are permanently write-protected. They have no open square notches on the left edge. This means that you cannot delete any files from them with the ERASE command. The copy of the DOS disk you made in Lesson 11, however, is not write-protected, so you can erase files from it. Again make sure that your DOS Startup disk copy is in drive A, and enter this command to erase the FORMAT.COM file:

erase format.com

Now enter this directory command to see what you've done:

dir format.com

The file is now gone, so your screen should look like Figure 2.16.

Figure 2.16 Erasing a File

```
A>erase format.com

A>dir format.com

 Volume in drive A has no label
 Directory of  A:\

File not found

A>_
```

Step 2: Erasing Several Files All at Once

By using the global file name characters * and ?, you can tell DOS to erase several files with a single ERASE command. In fact, you can even wipe out every file on the whole disk. Although this is often useful to clear off a disk, it should be used with care. Make sure that your DOS Startup disk copy is in drive A, and enter this command:

erase *.*

Because this is a potentially disastrous command if entered by mistake, DOS will ask you if you're sure you want to do this. If you enter **y** for yes, DOS will go ahead and erase everything. If you say **n** for no, DOS will immediately cancel the ERASE command. You will only get this chance to back out, however, if you use the *.* designation. If you enter **erase *.exe**, DOS does not ask you if you're sure and immediately deletes all files with an extension of EXE. So again, *be careful* with the ERASE command!

Answer **y** to erase all the files and enter **dir** to examine the disk directory. Your screen should look like Figure 2.17.

Lesson 14: Displaying a Text File

So far, you've learned quite a bit about manipulating files with DOS. You haven't, however, yet looked inside one. The DOS TYPE command lets you display the contents of a file on the screen. Although TYPE will work with almost any file, unless it's a text file all you'll see is gibberish on the screen. A text file is one that is produced by a text editor or word processing program. Unfortunately, none of the files on the DOS disks are text files; they are all program files or system files. So, for the next two lessons we're going to use an interesting application of the COPY command to create a sample text file. Then we'll show you how to display that file on your screen and print it out.

Figure 2.17 Erasing All the Files

```
A>erase *.*
Are you sure (Y/N)?y

A>dir

 Volume in drive A has no label
 Directory of  A:\

File not found

A>_
```

Step 1: Create a Sample Text File

DOS has an interesting feature that lets you treat certain devices, such as the keyboard/screen combination or the printer, as if they were files. These devices are given reserved names that you can use as if they were file names. For example, the keyboard and screen together are given the reserved name CON, which stands for console. Similarly, the primary printer connected to the computer can be referred to as PRN. You can use these *device names* in DOS commands as if they were file names.

We're going to use this feature along with the COPY command to create a text file. Put the new diskette you first formatted in Lesson 8 into disk drive A and enter this command:

copy con readme.txt

This command tells DOS to take everything you now type at the keyboard and copy it into a new file named README.TXT. Type the following text, pressing the **Enter** key at the end of each line:

This is a sample text file created to demonstrate the
use of the DOS TYPE and PRINT commands. A text file is
simply a file that contains only letters, numbers,
punctuation marks, and other symbols that appear on the
keyboard. Normally, text files are created with a text
editor or word processing program. You can, however,
create small text files directly from DOS by using the
COPY command with the device name CON. When you are
finished entering text, you must press the F6 function
key and then the Enter key to generate an end-of-file
code and have DOS copy the text file to your disk.

As the paragraph says, when you are finished entering the last line, press the **F6** function key and then press the **Enter** key. This inserts the DOS end-of-file code and completes the COPY command. Now enter **dir** to confirm that you have created the file on your disk. At this point, your screen should look like Figure 2.18.

Figure 2.18 Creating a Text File

```
A>copy con readme.txt
This is a sample text file created to demonstrate the
use of the DOS TYPE and PRINT commands.  A text file is
simply a file that contains only letters, numbers,
punctuation marks, and other symbols that appear on the
keyboard.  Normally, text files are created with a text
editor or word processing program.  You can, however,
create small text files directly from DOS by using the
COPY command with the device name CON.  When you are
finished entering text, you must press the F6 function
key and then the Enter key to generate an end-of-file
code and have DOS copy the text file to your disk.
^Z
        1 File(s) copied

A>dir

 Volume in drive A has no label
 Directory of  A:\

README   TXT       595   7-14-88  11:54a
        1 File(s)    308224 bytes free

A>_
```

Step 2: Issue the TYPE Command

There's now a file named README.TXT on your disk in drive A. You can see the contents of this file by using the DOS TYPE command. To use the TYPE command, simply enter **type** followed by the name of the file you wish to display. Enter this command to see what's in the file README.TXT:

type readme.txt

DOS will then display the contents of README.TXT on your screen, as shown in Figure 2.19.

Figure 2.19 Displaying a Text File

```
A>type readme.txt
This is a sample text file created to demonstrate the
use of the DOS TYPE and PRINT commands.  A text file is
simply a file that contains only letters, numbers,
punctuation marks, and other symbols that appear on the
keyboard.  Normally, text files are created with a text
editor or word processing program.  You can, however,
create small text files directly from DOS by using the
COPY command with the device name CON.  When you are
finished entering text, you must press the F6 function
key and then the Enter key to generate an end-of-file
code and have DOS copy the text file to your disk.

A>_
```

Lesson 15: Printing a Text File

Most text files eventually wind up on paper; after all, the end product of word processing is usually a hard copy document. The DOS PRINT command lets you send a text file directly to the printer, instead of displaying it on the screen. You'll need a printer for this lesson, as well as the diskette with the README.TXT file you created in Lesson 14.

Step 1: Put the DOS Operating Disk in Drive A

Unlike TYPE, the PRINT command is an external command that resides on the DOS Operating diskette. (DOS versions prior to 3.30 have the PRINT command on the diskette labeled DOS.) So, you must first put the disk containing the PRINT command into drive A. If your computer has two floppy drives, put the disk containing README.TXT in drive B.

Step 2: Turn on Your Printer

Before you can print a file, your printer must be turned on. Make sure that the power is on and that the printer is on-line, that is, connected to your computer.

Step 3: Issue the PRINT Command

To use the PRINT command, just type PRINT followed by the name of the file you want to print. You can preface the name of the file by the letter of the disk drive on which it is stored. Even if your computer has only one floppy drive, enter this command:

print b:readme.txt

After you do this, DOS will ask you to supply the following:

```
Name of list device [PRN]:
```

This rather cryptic request allows you to tell DOS which printer to use if you have more than one connected to your computer. The expression [PRN] means that unless you tell it otherwise, DOS will send the output to the default printer, which has the device name PRN. If you have only one printer, then it is the default printer. All you have to do here is just press the **Enter** key. DOS will ask you to supply the list device only the first time you use PRINT for any given computer session.

If you have a B floppy drive in your computer, PRINT will inform you that it's currently printing README.TXT and your printer should be merrily pounding away (unless, of course, it's a laser or ink-jet printer). Figure 2.20 shows what you should see on your screen.

If your computer only has one floppy drive, then DOS will ask you to do the following:

```
Insert diskette for drive B: and strike any key when ready.
```

Figure 2.20 Printing a Text File

```
A>print b:readme.txt
Name of list device [PRN]:
Resident part of PRINT installed

    B:\README.TXT is currently being printed

A>_
```

This is an example of a handy DOS feature. If you have only an A drive, and you issue a command that refers to drive B, DOS will temporarily pretend that drive A is drive B. It will then ask you to insert into drive A the disk you would have put into drive B if you had a drive B. So, if you have only one floppy drive, put the README.TXT disk in drive A when you get this message and press any key to finish the printing process.

The end result of this PRINT command will be a printout of the text in file README.TXT that you saw on your screen when you used the TYPE command in Lesson 14.

Lesson 16: Running a Program

This lesson won't really teach you anything new, because you've been running programs throughout this entire chapter. Every time you entered a DOS command, you were running a program. Remember: files with an EXE or COM extension are executable programs that you can run.

Step 1: Insert the Appropriate Disk

Just as you have to put the appropriate DOS disk in drive A when you want to use an external command, you must make sure a program is stored on a disk in one of your drives when you want to run the program. For example, to run an application program such as VP-Expert, you must have its disk in the A or B drive. Or, if your computer has a hard disk, you could run the program off the C drive provided that a copy resides there. If your computer is connected to a local area network, you could run the program if it's stored on your network's server disk. DOS must be able to find a program before it can be run.

Step 2: Switch to the Appropriate Drive, if Necessary

For example, if you have two floppy drives, the DOS disk in A, and the application's program disk in B, you could switch to drive B as you learned in Lesson 5. The alternative to switching drives is to preface the program name you enter with the letter of the drive on which the program's file is stored.

Step 3: Type the Program Name and Press the Enter Key

As you now know, you invoke an external DOS command by entering its name along with any necessary file names and other information. In this sense, application programs such as VP-Expert are the same as DOS external commands; all you have to do to run them is type the name of the EXE or COM file in which they're stored and press the **Enter** key. So, for example, to run the VP-Expert program off your current default drive, just type **vpx** and press the **Enter** key. Or, if your default drive is A and the VP-Expert disk is in drive B, you could enter **b:vpx** from the A drive to run the program. When you do either of these, DOS will load the VP-Expert program into primary memory and begin executing it.

Lesson 17: Working with Subdirectories

As you can imagine, people who use microcomputers extensively often generate large numbers of files. Before hard disks became common, users had many different floppy disks on which to store their files. Organizing files meant physically organizing diskettes by keeping them well-labeled and storing them in subdivided boxes, racks, or cabinets. Once hard disks became common, however, operating systems had to devise a better method of organizing large numbers of files. Even a modest 20-megabyte hard disk can store thousands of different files. Looking for a particular file among hundreds or thousands of files is time consuming and tedious. Consequently, most microcomputer operating systems, including DOS, have evolved a **hierarchical** method of organizing files into groups. Such a system allows you to cluster files into orders or ranks, each subordinate to the one above. These groups of files, called **subdirectories**, are like file folders that can be nested within one another. Disks can be organized into subdirectories, each of which can contain files and other subdirectories.

Subdirectories are invaluable tools for organizing programs and data files on high-capacity storage devices. In addition, subdirectories make it easier for the operating system to locate a particular file because large numbers of files are divided into smaller groups. Although subdirectories are most often, indeed almost always, found on hard disks, they are occasionally used on floppy disks, too. DOS includes commands that let you create, access, and remove subdirectories.

With DOS, every disk has a single main directory, known as the **root directory**. DOS automatically creates a root directory on every disk you format. This is the directory you are in when you first boot up DOS or when you first change your default drive. The root directory itself has no name, but it's represented by a backslash (\).

Step 1: Create a Subdirectory

Let's create a subdirectory on the new floppy disk you have used in previous lessons (the one with README.TXT on it). Put this disk into drive A, and enter this command:

md a:\text

The internal DOS command MD or MKDIR (short for Make Directory) is used to create a new subdirectory. It is followed by the **path** of the new subdirectory. The path is an optional disk drive specifier followed by a list of subdirectory names, separated by backslashes. The rules for naming subdirectories are the same as the rules for naming files. The simplest path is a single backslash \, which represents the root directory of your current default drive. The command you just entered creates a subdirectory named TEXT on the disk in drive A. This subdirectory is one level below the root directory.

Step 2: Change to the Subdirectory

Think of the subdirectory as a separate "sub-disk" on your disk. Enter **dir** to display a directory of your disk. Now enter the Change Directory (CD or CHDIR) command to move into your new subdirectory:

cd a:\text

Enter **dir** again and Figure 2.21 shows what you should see on your screen. The first DIR gives a directory listing of the root directory of the floppy disk. It contains the README.TXT file and the TEXT subdirectory. The second DIR gives a directory listing inside the TEXT subdirectory.

Figure 2.21 Changing to a Subdirectory

```
A>md a:\text

A>dir

 Volume in drive A has no label
 Directory of  A:\

README   TXT      595   7-14-88  11:54a
TEXT         <DIR>      7-14-88   2:31p
        2 File(s)    307200 bytes free

A>cd a:\text

A>dir

 Volume in drive A has no label
 Directory of  A:\TEXT

.            <DIR>      7-14-88   2:31p
..           <DIR>      7-14-88   2:31p
        2 File(s)    307200 bytes free

A>_
```

Step 3: Copy a File to the Subdirectory

Right now, the TEXT subdirectory has no ordinary user files in it. You can, however, copy your own files to this subdirectory just as if it were a separate disk. For example, let's copy the README.TXT file from the root directory to the TEXT subdirectory. Enter this command:

copy a:\readme.txt

This command copies the file README.TXT from the root directory of drive A to your current subdirectory, which happens to be TEXT. Now enter **dir** and you'll see that a copy of README.TXT now also exists in the TEXT subdirectory. It's important to realize that there are two separate copies of README.TXT now on the disk: one in the root directory and one in the TEXT subdirectory.

Step 4: Remove the Subdirectory

Once you're in a subdirectory, you can almost think of it as a separate disk. You can run programs from within a subdirectory. Many DOS commands that deal with files will operate only on the files in your current subdirectory unless you specify otherwise. For example, you can delete every file in a subdirectory without affecting any files in the root directory or any other subdirectories. For example, try entering this command:

erase *.*

Answer **y** for yes when the ERASE command asks if you are sure that this is what you want to do. DOS will erase every file in your current directory, the TEXT subdirectory. Enter **dir** to see that this is true. Now change back to the root directory by entering this command:

cd a:

Now enter another DIR command and you will see that the README.TXT file in the root is still intact.

Just as you must occasionally delete unneeded files, sometimes subdirectories must be removed, too. Let's say that you are finished with the TEXT subdirectory and you want to remove it from your disk. To do this you must first erase any files inside the subdirectory and move out of the subdirectory. We've already done this. Now you can enter the Remove Directory command (RD or RMDIR) to remove the empty TEXT subdirectory from your disk:

rd a:\text

If you enter **dir**, you will see that the TEXT subdirectory has indeed been removed, and your disk is the same as it was when you began this lesson.

Lesson 18: Using Batch Files

A **batch file** is a text file that contains a list of commands or programs to be run. Batch files are usually created with a text editor or word processing program, but you can easily create short ones using the COPY command method we outlined in Step 1 of Lesson 14. In DOS, every batch file must have an extension of BAT. Once it has been created, a batch file is invoked by typing its filename and pressing the **Enter** key. When this is done, DOS executes each command or program listed in the batch file, one at a time. DOS includes features that enable experienced users to construct complex and very helpful batch files. Even if you never actually make your own batch files, you will undoubtedly use some made by others or included with application packages. As an example, let's create and use a simple batch file.

Step 1: Create the Batch File

As we said, batch files are usually created with a text editor or word processor. Short ones, however, can be easily created with the COPY command. At this point, you should still have the floppy disk with the README.TXT file on it in drive A. Enter this command to create a new batch file named SHOW.BAT on your current disk:

copy con show.bat

Now you can enter the text that will go inside the file SHOW.BAT. Type the following three commands, pressing the **Enter** key after each one:

cls
dir
type readme.txt

Finally, press the **F6** function key to generate the end-of-file code and then press the **Enter** key. Enter **dir** to examine the current contents of your disk and see that the batch file has indeed been created. Your screen should look like Figure 2.22.

Figure 2.22 Creating a Batch File

```
A>copy con show.bat
cls
dir
type readme.txt
^Z
        1 File(s) copied

A>dir

 Volume in drive A has no label
 Directory of  A:\

README   TXT      595   7-14-88  11:54a
SHOW     BAT       27   7-15-88   9:14a
        2 File(s)    307200 bytes free

A>_
```

Step 2: Use the Batch File

Running a batch file is just like executing a command or running an application program. You type its filename (without the extension) and press the Enter key. To run your newly created batch file, simply type **show** and press the **Enter** key. Figure 2.23 shows the result.

Figure 2.23 Using a Batch File

```
A>dir

 Volume in drive A has no label
 Directory of  A:\

README   TXT      595   7-14-88  11:54a
SHOW     BAT       27   7-15-88   9:14a
        2 File(s)    307200 bytes free

A>type readme.txt
This is a sample text file created to demonstrate the
use of the DOS TYPE and PRINT commands.  A text file is
simply a file that contains only letters, numbers,
punctuation marks, and other symbols that appear on the
keyboard.  Normally, text files are created with a text
editor or word processing program.  You can, however,
create small text files directly from DOS by using the
COPY command with the device name CON.  When you are
finished entering text, you must press the F6 function
key and then the Enter key to generate an end-of-file
code and have DOS copy the text file to your disk.

A>
A>_
```

Most commands and programs that you can run directly from the DOS prompt can be put inside a batch file. Batch files allow you to automate frequently executed series of commands. They also allow experts to set up complex sequences of commands to be run by novices. For example, many new application programs must be installed on your system before you can use them. In some cases, this installation process can be quite involved. Most software developers, therefore, include one or more batch files that make the installation process much easier for users.

The AUTOEXEC.BAT File The most commonly used batch file is a special one named AUTOEXEC.BAT–the auto-execute batch file. Whenever you boot up your computer, DOS searches the root directory of the current drive for this AUTOEXEC.BAT file. If there is no AUTOEXEC.BAT file present, DOS simply asks you to supply the current date and time, and then presents its prompt. If, on the other hand, AUTOEXEC.BAT is found, then that batch file is automatically executed. Since the AUTOEXEC.BAT file is automatically invoked every time you boot up your computer, it is ideal for listing any commands and programs you always run when you first turn on your machine. For example, if there is a subdirectory that you always use, you could put a CD (Change Directory) command in the AUTOEXEC.BAT to move into that subdirectory. Most DOS users eventually set up their own AUTOEXEC.BAT files or have someone else help them do so.

Conclusion

In this chapter of the *Software Guide*, you've learned several of the most frequently used DOS commands. To be sure, we haven't covered every DOS command or discussed every feature of this rich and powerful operating system. Most computer users, however, find that they primarily spend their time running application programs such as VP-Expert. Their direct interaction with DOS is, for the most part, on the level of the commands and procedures we've introduced in this chapter. To learn even more about DOS, consult one of the many books completely devoted to the subject. Or, refer to the documentation provided by IBM and Microsoft: the *DOS User's Guide* and the *DOS Reference* manual.

Exercises

Multiple Choice

Choose the best selection to complete each statement.

______ 1. An operating system is a(n)
   a. hardware component of a mainframe computer system.
   b. application program that produces text files.
   c. set of programs that lets you use your computer's hardware and software resources.
   d. system of procedures for operating a computer.

______ 2. Transient routines or external commands are
   (a) kept in primary memory until the computer is shut off.
   (b) kept on disk and loaded into memory only when needed.
   (c) kept in ROM (read-only memory) chips.
   (d) used once then deleted.

______ 3. The driving force behind each new DOS release has usually been
   (a) the addition of a new disk drive capability.
   (b) an effort to improve the user interface.
   (c) an attempt to eliminate all bugs.
   (d) an effort by IBM and Microsoft to make more money.

______ 4. Upwardly compatible means that
   (a) you cannot take advantage of the new version's abilities.
   (b) all old software versions must be upgraded.
   (c) new hardware must be purchased to use the new version.
   (d) operations that worked with former versions work with the new version.

______ 5. A command is a(n)
   (a) combination of hardware switch settings.
   (b) operating system directive issued to a user.
   (c) application package instruction.
   (d) word or abbreviation that tells DOS to run a program.

______ 6. To boot DOS with the power off
   (a) insert the DOS disk and turn on the power.
   (b) hold down the Control, Alternate, and Delete keys at the same time.
   (c) turn the power on and issue the boot command.
   (d) turn the power on and kick the computer.

______ 7. Pressing Ctrl-Alt-Del will
   (a) invoke a DOS transient routine.
   (b) delete a file.
   (c) reboot DOS without having to shut off the computer.
   (d) execute an application program.

______ 8. The DOS directory command is
   (a) DIRECT.
   (b) LIST.
   (c) DIR.
   (d) CATALOG.

______ 9. The two parts of a DOS file name are
   (a) a disk drive designation and a disk sector number.
   (b) a primary file name and an optional extension.
   (c) a primary file name and a creation date.
   (d) a primary extension and the size in bytes.

__________ 10. Files with COM and EXE extensions usually designate
(a) external commands and executable program files.
(b) command files and extension files.
(c) configuration files and batch files.
(d) BASIC and FORTRAN files.

__________ 11. Pressing Ctrl-Num Lock or Pause will
(a) echo input and output to the printer.
(b) print the screen.
(c) cancel a command.
(d) temporarily halt screen scrolling.

__________ 12. To change the default disk drive
(a) put a new disk in drive A.
(b) type the new disk drive designation and press **Enter**.
(c) open up the computer and replace the faulty drive.
(d) issue the DIR command.

__________ 13. To display a disk and memory status report, enter
(a) status.
(b) dir.
(c) chkdsk.
(d) diskcopy.

__________ 14. Formatting a diskette does not
(a) check the diskette for bad sectors.
(b) wipe out all data on the diskette.
(c) mark off the space into sectors.
(d) sort files in the directory.

__________ 15. To format a system diskette you must
(a) reboot the system.
(b) use the /s parameter with the FORMAT command.
(c) enter the COPY command.
(d) purchase a master diskette from IBM.

__________ 16. One way to copy every file from disk drive A to B is to
(a) enter copy a:*.* b:.
(b) enter dir a: b:.
(c) enter copy a: b:.
(d) use the REN command.

__________ 17. To make an exact copy of an entire diskette, use
(a) COPY.
(b) DISKCOPY.
(c) DIR.
(d) Ctrl-Alt-Del.

__________ 18. Entering the command del *.* will
(a) reboot the system.
(b) copy all files to the disk in the default drive.
(c) rename all files on the disk in the default drive.
(d) erase all files from the disk in the default drive.

__________ 19. To display a text file on your screen use the
(a) PRINT command.
(b) DISKCOPY command.
(c) TYPE command.
(d) Ctrl-Num Lock key.

__________ 20. To run a program or batch file you must
(a) type its filename and press the Enter key.
(b) reboot DOS.
(c) press Ctrl-Break.
(d) first make a backup copy.

Fill-In

1. A disk operating system has many utilities for dealing with the ______________ that are stored on disks.

2. ______________ is usually used with IBM computers while ______________ is usually used with compatible computers such as those made by Compaq, AT&T, Tandy, and Zenith.

3. Booting DOS refers to the process of loading the disk operating system into ____________.

4. In many cases, when you first boot DOS it asks you to enter the ____________ and the ____________.

5. The ____________ command can be used to list the names, sizes, and creation dates and times of all the files on a disk.

6. A file's primary filename can have from one to ____________ characters in it.

7. File name extensions are often used to ____________ files.

8. You can press the ____________ key to cancel a command if you haven't pressed the Enter key yet.

9. You can press ____________ to cancel a command before it finishes normally.

10. The DOS ____________ indicates the current default disk drive.

11. The ____________ command can tell you how much memory is installed in your computer.

12. A diskette must be ____________ before it can be used to store program and data files.

13. The ____________ command can be used to duplicate one or more files on the same or on different disks.

14. ____________ file name characters can be used to refer to several files at the same time.

15. The DISKCOPY command will automatically ____________ the target diskette if it's brand new.

16. The REN command can be used to ____________ one or more file names.

17. To remove a file from a disk, you would enter ____________ or ____________ followed by the file's name.

18. The TYPE command lets you display ____________ files on your screen.

19. You could use the ____________ command to produce a hard copy of a text file.

20. The DOS commands used to create, change to, and remove subdirectories are ____________, ____________, and ____________.

Short Problems

1. If you have access to a diskette other than the DOS floppies, produce a directory listing of the files on it. If you have a printer, try using Ctrl-PrtSc to turn on printer echoing before you issue the directory command so that you can get a hard copy.

2. When you booted DOS, you were asked to supply the date and time. Two DOS commands, DATE and TIME, tell you the current date and time and let you change these settings. Try the DATE and TIME commands. If you don't want to change the date and time settings, just press the **Enter** key when asked for the new date or time. Notice how DOS automatically figures out and displays the day of the week.

3. Use the * global file name character to produce a directory listing of all the files on the DOS Startup disk with an EXE extension.

4. Use the * global file name character to produce a directory listing of all the files on the DOS Startup disk whose names begin with the letter K.

5. Use the ? global file name character to produce a directory listing of all the files on the DOS Startup disk that have an E as the second letter of their primary filenames.

6. You've probably noticed the "Volume in drive A has no label" message DOS gives when it displays a directory of the DOS disk. The FORMAT command has an option that lets you specify a name for a disk, or volume label as DOS calls it. Try formatting a blank disk with this command:

   format b:/v

   If you have only one floppy drive, enter this instead:

   format a:/v

   The /V is an optional parameter that tells the FORMAT command to ask you for a volume label. Think up a name of 11 characters or less and enter it when FORMAT tells you to. When you're done, check the disk's directory to see your volume label displayed.

7. DOS versions 3.0 and newer have a command that lets you supply or change a volume label without having to reformat a disk. If you have DOS 3.0 or newer try using the LABEL command on the new disk you've just formatted. Note that you can't change the label of the original DOS disk because it's write-protected.

8. If you don't know what DOS version you have, enter **ver**. This command displays the number of the DOS version you are using.

9. Another way to find out the volume label of a disk is to use the VOL command. Enter **vol a:**. This command displays the volume label (if there is one) of the disk in drive A.

10. It is possible to display a text file on your screen by using the COPY command instead of the TYPE command. In certain cases, DOS can refer to its peripheral devices as if they were files. There are several file names that have a special meaning to DOS. These are called DOS device names. For example, CON refers to the console, or the keyboard and screen. Put the disk with your README.TXT file in drive A and enter this command:

    copy readme.txt con

    You should see the text of file README.TXT displayed on your screen just as if you used the TYPE command.

11. Just as CON is a DOS device name that refers to the keyboard and screen, PRN is a DOS device name that refers to the printer. Try using the COPY command to get a printout of the README.TXT file.

12. The DIR command has two optional parameters that can be useful when looking at disks with lots of files on them. The /P parameter will automatically pause the display when the screen is full and let you press a key to continue. The /W parameter will display the directory in a wide format across the screen, omitting the sizes and creation dates and times so that more file names will fit at once. Put your DOS Startup disk in drive A and try entering these options:

    dir /p
    dir /w

3

Expert Systems: VP-Expert

Learning Objectives

By the end of this chapter, you should be able to do the following:

- Invoke the VP-Expert program
- Use the VP-Expert menus
- Use the VP-Expert Help facility
- Use the VP-Expert Editor
- Create a knowledge base by entering its rules
- Run a consultation
- Understand backward chaining
- Use variables with multiple values
- Use rules with multiple conditions
- Create a knowledge base from an induction table
- Enhance the appearance of a consultation
- Use all options of the Consult menu

Introduction

An **expert system** is a computer program that contains a collection of facts and a list of rules for making inferences about those facts. The facts and rules usually concern one particular field and are generally contributed by experts in that field. Expert systems use those facts and rules to advise, analyze, categorize, diagnose, explain, identify, interpret, and teach. They attempt to address problems traditionally solved by human experts. A few of the many expert systems now in use are MYCIN, which helps doctors to diagnose infections; PROSPECTOR, which aids geologists in evaluating mineral sites; and TAXADVISOR, which gives estate-planning advice.

Expert systems are among the most useful and marketable products of **artificial intelligence**. This intriguing field of study combines aspects of computer science, mathematics, philosophy, psychology, and linguistics. The main goal of artificial intelligence research is to enable computers to mimic certain aspects of human learning and decision-making.

The expert system examples we've just mentioned are quite specific, and many expert systems run only on minicomputers or mainframes. Special artificial intelligence programming languages, such as LISP and PROLOG, are frequently used to develop proprietary expert systems. There is, however, a relatively new class of software that runs on microcomputers and lets nonprogrammers set up their own expert systems. These programs are called expert system shells.

An **expert system shell** is an application package that contains everything you need to create your own expert systems and is easier to use than a programming language such as LISP or PROLOG. You supply the facts to create the knowledge base and the rules to create the rule base. The expert system shell contains the inference engine, which actually applies your facts and rules to answer questions or give advice to the user, or client. If necessary, the inference engine asks its own questions to get additional information. The inference engine then uses simple logic to draw conclusions from the details of a particular situation. Many expert system shells can also explain, with text and graphics, exactly how their conclusions have been reached.

One of the most popular expert system shells for microcomputers is VP-Expert, from Paperback Software International. With a retail price less than $200, VP-Expert provides an economical way to develop simple expert systems. The program helps you with all the steps needed to create a complete expert system, from entering the knowledge base to specifying the details of a typical consultation session with a client. Once you enter the facts that comprise the knowledge base, VP-Expert can analyze the data and automatically derive a preliminary set of rules to govern those data. You can examine this rule base and modify or supplement it as needed. Then the program lets you test the expert system by seeing how it behaves when a client asks a question.

Multiple windows take you through a simulated consultation session. One window displays the rules as they are being tested. Another window shows the conclusions that have been reached so far. A third window lists the questions that the client would be asked. In an actual session, the client would have to answer those questions. When the simulated consultation session is finished, VP-Expert can display a graphical tree that shows the complete reasoning path that was followed to reach the conclusions. VP-Expert also lets you assign a **confidence factor** from 0 to 100 to an answer that isn't simply yes or no. Once the expert system has been thoroughly tested in this manner, it can be used for consultation by clients.

General Features of VP-Expert

VP-Expert is an easy-to-use, economical, yet powerful expert system shell. Although the package includes an impressive set of sophisticated features, it can be used by beginners on a more modest level. In this chapter, we'll concentrate on VP-Expert's most fundamental features. Some of the things you can do with VP-Expert include:

- **Using Menus** VP-Expert has an excellent system of menus for selecting commands and options. You can highlight an item, press its first letter, or press a corresponding number or function key to make a choice.
- **Getting Help** Specific information about the current activity can be obtained by pressing the F1 key from most menus. A comprehensive help index lets you get a description of any VP-Expert feature.
- **Editing Files** The integrated VP-Expert Editor lets you create and modify knowledge base and induction table files without leaving the program.
- **Creating a Knowledge Base** You can create a knowledge base directly by entering ACTIONS, rules, and statements.
- **Consulting a Knowledge Base** Once a knowledge base has been set up, you can consult it to help answer a question.
- **Using Backward Chaining** VP-Expert uses a sophisticated problem-solving technique called backward chaining to try to find an answer to your question.
- **Getting Multiple Answers** VP-Expert can answer certain questions with more than one response.
- **Using Multiple Conditions** VP-Expert can handle complex situations with multiple conditions.

- **Using Induction** You can have VP-Expert automatically create a complete expert system from a table of facts.
- **Enhancing Consultations** Various commands let you govern the appearance of the screen during a consultation session.
- **Controlling Consultations** The Consult menu has several options that let you control various aspects of consulting a knowledge base.

Getting Started

Although VP-Expert is a powerful tool, it's easy to use. The package has a well-written manual and an excellent built-in help facility. In this guide, we'll be using VP-Expert Version 2.0, but most of what we do will also work with earlier versions. The program comes from Paperback Software on two floppy disks: the Program disk and the Sample Files disk. The three most likely arrangements for students running VP-Expert are

1. on a computer with two floppy drives and the VP-Expert package on the two floppy disks
2. on a computer with a hard disk and at least one floppy disk drive, with the VP-Expert package installed on the hard disk in a subdirectory named VPX or VPEXPERT
3. on a computer connected to a local area network, with the VP-Expert package installed on the network's file server

In each of these cases, the computer may be any IBM-compatible. Because computer systems can be organized in many ways, your instructor might have you follow some directions unique to your particular installation. Once you are running VP-Expert, however, you should be able to work all of the following lessons.

Lesson 1: Running VP-Expert

Like any software package, VP-Expert must be loaded into your computer's memory before you can use it. So, the first thing to do is gain access to and run the VP-Expert program.

Step 1: Boot Up DOS

If your computer isn't already turned on and running DOS, you'll need to boot it up. On computer systems with only two floppy drives, put your DOS disk in drive A, close the door or lever if you have one, and turn on the system unit. If your computer has a hard disk drive or is connected to a local area network, just turn it on. Don't forget to turn on your display if it is a color monitor. Finally, enter the date and time (if necessary) to complete the DOS boot-up process as we described in Lesson 1 of Chapter 1.

Step 2: Change the Disk or Subdirectory

If your computer has only two floppy drives, remove the DOS disk from drive A, replace it with the VP-Expert Program Disk, and insert the Sample Files disk into drive B.

If you are using a hard disk drive or a network, you may need to follow some other directions from your instructor in order to use VP-Expert. For example, if

VP-Expert is installed on your hard disk in a subdirectory named VPEXPERT, you may need to switch to that subdirectory by entering this DOS command:

```
cd \vpexpert
```

Step 3: Invoke VP-Expert

Once you get situated in the proper disk drive and directory, running VP-Expert is easy. Type **vpx** and press **Enter**. Figure 3.1 shows the copyright message and Main menu that appear on your screen.

Figure 3.1 VP-Expert Version 2.0 Copyright Screen and Main Menu

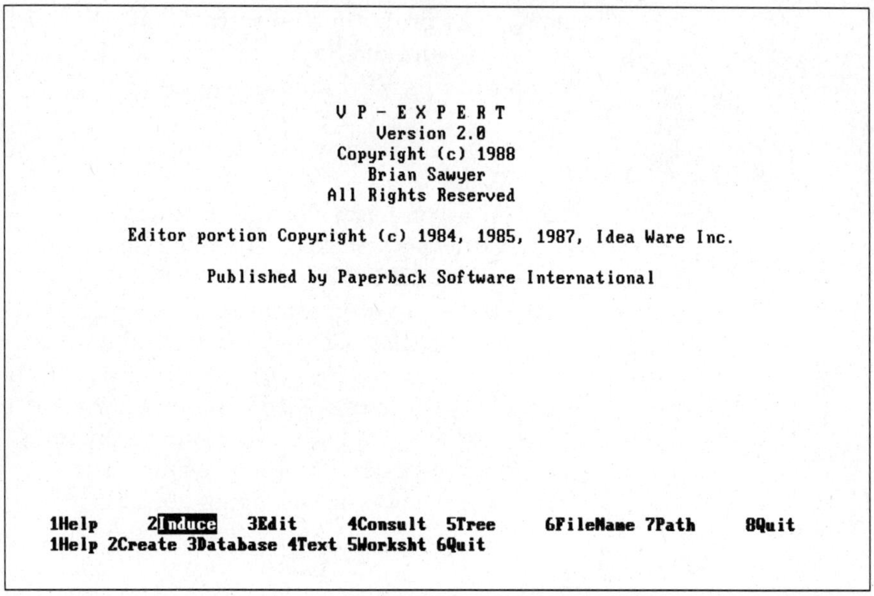

```
                         V P - E X P E R T
                            Version 2.0
                         Copyright (c) 1988
                            Brian Sawyer
                        All Rights Reserved

        Editor portion Copyright (c) 1984, 1985, 1987, Idea Ware Inc.

              Published by Paperback Software International

1Help     2Induce    3Edit     4Consult  5Tree      6FileName 7Path     8Quit
1Help 2Create 3Database 4Text 5Worksht 6Quit
```

Step 4: Use the Main Menu

VP-Expert's Main menu is similar to those found in many popular application packages. You can select an option from the menu in any one of four ways:

- Press the Right Arrow or Left Arrow key to move the highlight bar to the desired option. The line of text below the menu will reveal a submenu or description of the option. Press Enter to actually execute it.
- Type the number preceding the option.
- Press the function key corresponding to the number preceding the option.
- Type the option's first letter, in either lowercase or uppercase.

For example, activate the Help facility by typing **1** or **h**, pressing **F1**, or pressing **Left Arrow** and then **Enter**. If you are working from a hard disk, Figure 3.2 will appear on your screen.

If your computer has only two floppy drives and you are working from the Program disk in drive A, VP-Expert will prompt you to insert the Sample Files disk in drive B and press **Enter**. The help facility is stored on the Sample Files disk. Make sure that the Sample Files disk is in drive B and press **Enter**. Now, your screen should look like Figure 3.2.

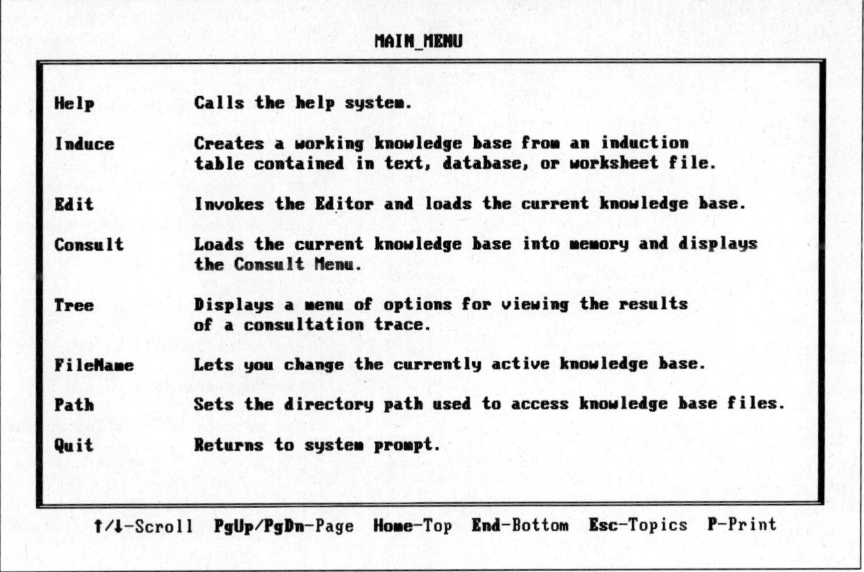

Figure 3.2 VP-Expert Main Menu Help Screen

Step 5: Explore the Help Facility

As Figure 3.2 shows, your screen reveals helpful information about the options in VP-Expert's Main menu. The line of text at the bottom of the screen tells you which keys to press for further help. For example, press **Escape** to see an index of all the topics you can look up. Your screen should look like Figure 3.3. Press **Page Up, Page Down, Up Arrow**, or **Down Arrow** to see more topics. Find *Function Keys* in the list of topics, highlight it with an arrow key, and press **Enter**. As Figure 3.4 shows, VP-Expert reveals the purpose of each function key. By providing such information about all commands, the Help facility makes VP-Expert easier to use and can often save you the trouble of referring to the printed manual. Press **Escape** twice to return to the Main menu.

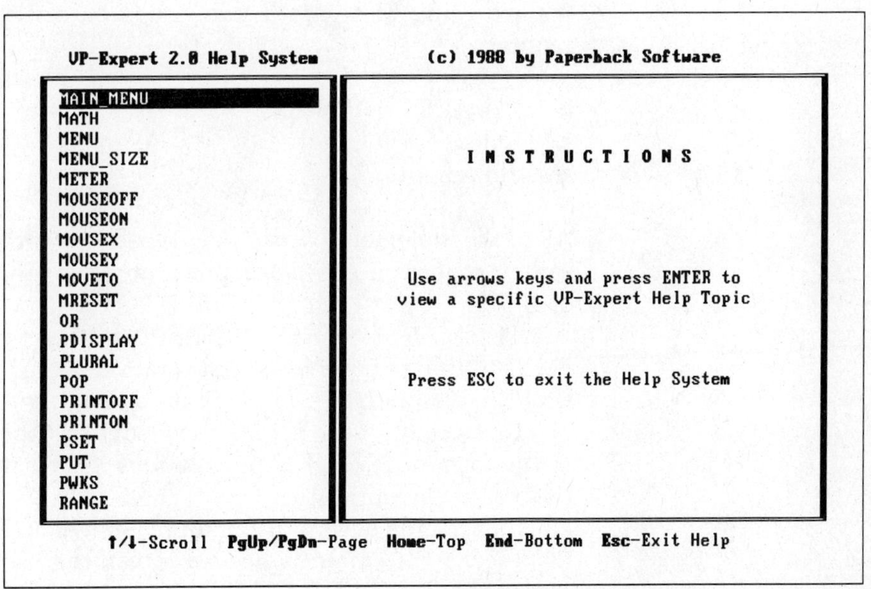

Figure 3.3 VP-Expert Help Index of Topics

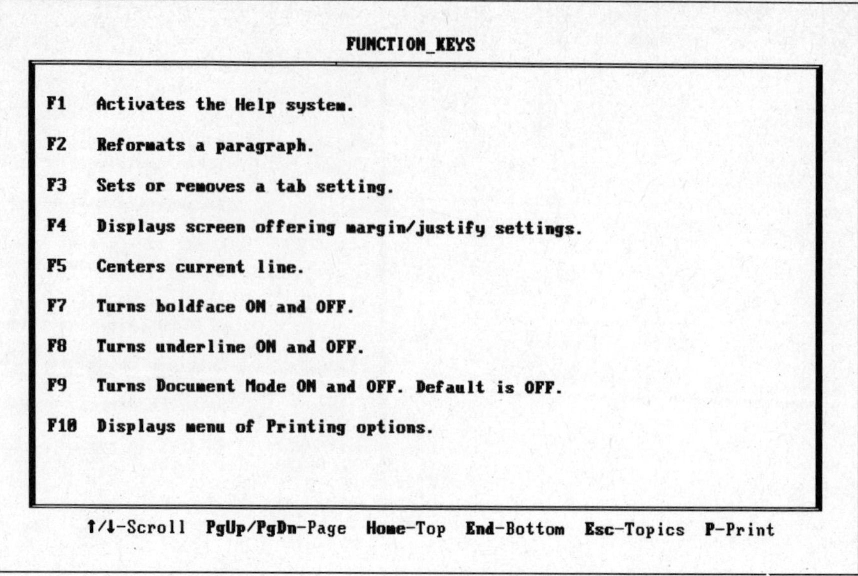
FUNCTION_KEYS

F1 Activates the Help system.
F2 Reformats a paragraph.
F3 Sets or removes a tab setting.
F4 Displays screen offering margin/justify settings.
F5 Centers current line.
F7 Turns boldface ON and OFF.
F8 Turns underline ON and OFF.
F9 Turns Document Mode ON and OFF. Default is OFF.
F10 Displays menu of Printing options.

↑/↓-Scroll PgUp/PgDn-Page Home-Top End-Bottom Esc-Topics P-Print

Figure 3.4 Function Key Help Screen

Step 6: Quit VP-Expert

Your screen should now contain only the Main menu—like Figure 3.1 without the copyright information in the middle. To try another VP-Expert command, let's exit the program and return to DOS. Type **q**. VP-Expert will terminate and the computer will present the DOS prompt. Don't worry, we'll start up VP-Expert again in the next lesson.

Lesson 2: Using the VP-Expert Editor

In this lesson we are going to use the VP-Expert editor to create a very simple expert system to give advice about removing stains from fabrics. More specifically, we are going to create a knowledge base file, which consists of three basic elements:

- The ACTIONS block
- Rules
- Statements

All of these elements are simply typed into an ordinary text file, somewhat like the source code of a computer program in a programming language such as Pascal or C.

The ACTIONS block defines the goal of the expert system by telling it what it needs to find out. In our stain removal expert system, the goal is to find a solvent that can dissolve the stain without damaging the fabric.

Rules contain the actual knowledge or expertise of the system. They are stated in the form of IF-THEN propositions. For example, IF the stain is coffee, THEN the solvent is cool water.

Statements control the manner in which a consultation session proceeds. For instance, a statement is needed to ask the user the composition of the stain to be removed.

Like a programming language, VP-Expert has specific formatting and punctuation guidelines for the entry of the ACTIONS, rules, and statements that make up a knowledge base file. These procedures, however, are fairly simple and straightforward.

Step 1: Start VP-Expert

If you are not already running VP-Expert, switch to the proper disk drive and subdirectory, type **vpx** and press **Enter**.

Step 2: Execute the Edit Option

Press **e** to invoke the Edit option from the Main menu. As Figure 3.5 shows, VP-Expert will ask you for the name of the knowledge base you want to use. The horizontal list across the bottom of the screen gives the names of knowledge base files already on your disk. Paperback Software provides several knowledge base files that are discussed as examples in the VP-Expert manual.

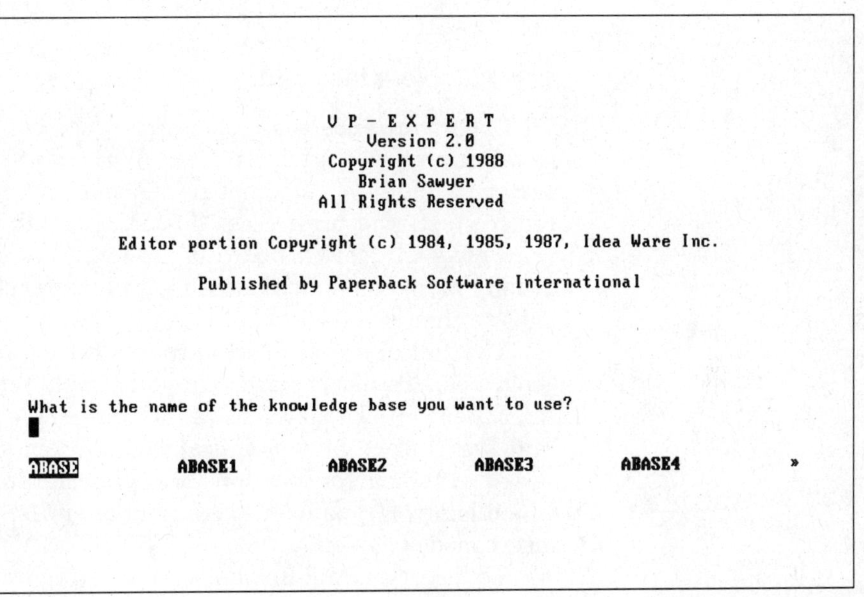

Figure 3.5 VP-Expert Asks for the Name of the File To Be Edited

Step 3: Enter a New File Name

We want to create a new knowledge base file, so instead of selecting an existing name, type **stains** and press **Enter**. VP-Expert will present the blank editing screen shown in Figure 3.6.

Figure 3.6 The VP-Expert Editor

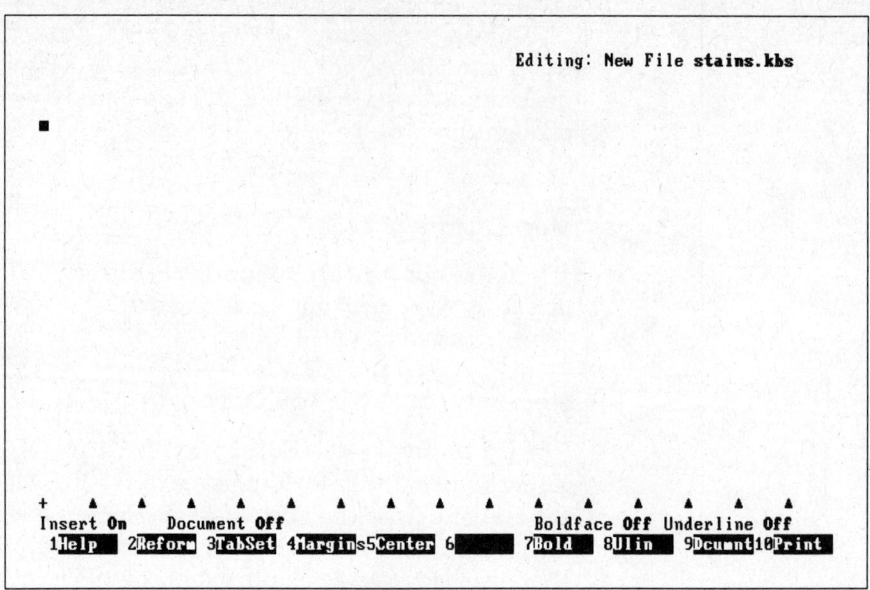

Step 4: Explore the Editor

VP-Expert includes a simple word processor, called the Editor, for entering and modifying knowledge base files. With it you can create and save files, move the cursor, delete text, reformat paragraphs, manipulate blocks of text, search for and replace text, and print files. In fact, you can create knowledge base files with any word processing or text editing program, but using the built-in VP-Expert Editor is usually more convenient because you don't have to exit VP-Expert every time you have to change a file.

The Editor's commands are similar to those found in many word processing programs. To insert new text, you simply type it. To begin a new line, you press the Enter key. Table 3.1 shows which keys let you move the cursor within the current file. Insert mode is initially turned on, so any characters you type will be inserted at the cursor location. Pressing the Insert key switches to overwrite mode, which lets you type over existing characters. Pressing the Insert key again turns insert mode back on.

To insert a blank line between existing lines of text, you move the cursor to the left edge of the screen and press Ctrl-Enter. The following keys let you delete text:

Delete	Character at the cursor
Backspace	Character to the left of the cursor
Ctrl-T	Word at the cursor
Ctrl-Y	Entire line

In addition to these basic operations, you use the function keys alone and with the Shift, Control (Ctrl), and Alternate (Alt) keys to execute most other Editor commands. We won't discuss all of the Editor's commands; you can use the Help facility or read the VP-Expert manual if you are interested. Table 3.2 lists the commands you will probably need most often.

Table 3.1 Cursor Movement Keys

Keypress	Cursor Movement
Up Arrow	Up one line
Down Arrow	Down one line
Left Arrow	Left one character
Right Arrow	Right one character
Ctrl-Left Arrow	Left one word
Ctrl-Right Arrow	Right one word
Home	Beginning of line
End	End of line
Tab	Forward one tab stop
Shift-Tab	Back one tab stop
Page Up	Previous screen
Page Down	Next screen
Ctrl-Page Up	Beginning of file
Ctrl-Page Down	End of file

Table 3.2 Commonly-Used Commands

Keypress	Command
F1	Invokes the Help facility
F10	Prints the file
Alt-F4	Inserts another file at the cursor location
Alt-F5	Saves the file to the disk without leaving the Editor
Alt-F6	Saves the file and leaves the Editor
Alt-F8	Leaves the Editor without saving the file
Ctrl-F3	Marks the beginning of a block
Ctrl-F4	Marks the end of a block
Ctrl-F5	Unmarks a marked block
Ctrl-F6	Moves a marked block to the current cursor location
Ctrl-F7	Copies a marked block to the current cursor location
Ctrl-F8	Deletes the marked block (the cursor must be inside the block)
Ctrl-F10	Restores the most recently deleted word, line, or block.

Lesson 3: Creating a Simple Knowledge Base

Our first knowledge base will be short and simple. It will give advice about removing three types of stains. We will expand on this modest knowledge base in later lessons as we explore more complex features of VP-Expert.

We will use the VP-Expert Editor to create our knowledge base. We've already chosen STAINS as the name of the file in Step 3 of the previous lesson. When you save the file at the end of this lesson, VP-Expert will automatically add the extension .KBS to STAINS, identifying the file as a knowledge base.

Step 1: Enter the ACTIONS Block

The first element in a knowledge base is the ACTIONS block. This consists of the keyword ACTIONS followed by one or more clauses and a semicolon. A **keyword** is a reserved word that has a special meaning to VP-Expert. See the Command Summary on the inside of the back cover of this guide for a list of some VP-Expert keywords. You cannot use any keyword to name your own item in a knowledge base. Although it is not required, keywords are customarily entered in uppercase letters. A **clause** is simply an instruction that makes up part of an ACTIONS block or rule. The clauses within an ACTIONS block tell VP-Expert the goals of your knowledge base. In our example, there is currently only one goal: to find the appropriate solvent to remove a particular stain. Enter the following lines to complete the ACTIONS block (you can press the **Tab** key to indent the word FIND):

```
ACTIONS
     FIND solvent;
```

Your screen should now look like Figure 3.7. The left arrowhead at the end of each line symbolizes the carriage return generated when you pressed the Enter key.

Figure 3.7 The ACTIONS Block

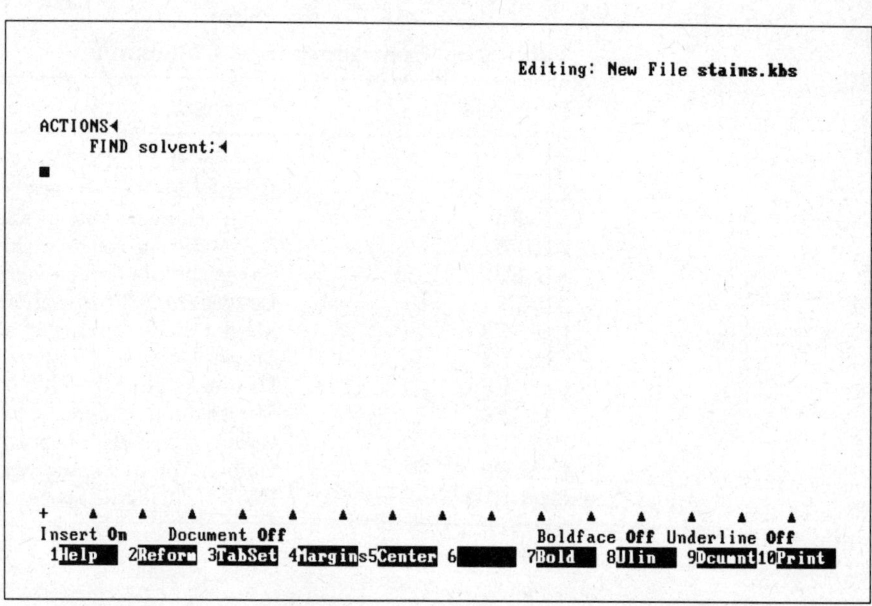

FIND is another VP-Expert keyword and *solvent* is a variable. A **variable** is a named storage area for holding a value. You make up the names of your variables when you use them. This particular FIND clause tells VP-Expert that the purpose of this knowledge base is to determine the appropriate solvent. The semicolon marks the end of the ACTIONS block.

Step 2: Enter the Rules

Rules contain the knowledge of the knowledge base and are expressed as IF-THEN propositions. For example, press **Enter** and then enter the following lines to create the first rule:

```
RULE 1
IF   stain = catsup
THEN solvent = dry_cleaning_fluid;
```

VP-Expert rules have four essential parts.

- The rule name
- The rule premise
- The rule conclusion
- A semicolon at the end of the rule

Each rule must begin with the keyword RULE followed by a space and a name between 1 and 40 characters long. Numbers are often used for rule names, especially in knowledge bases with many rules. For instance, the name of the rule you just entered is simply 1. In addition to letters and numbers, the following characters are also allowed in rule names:

```
_ $ % ^ |
```

The rule premise begins with the keyword IF. Up to twenty conditions can be stated in the premise. A **condition** compares the contents of a variable to a value. In our rule premise, there is only one condition, *stain = catsup*. *Stain* is the variable, *catsup* is the value, and = is the **relational operator**, which is a symbol specifying the type of comparison to be performed. VP-Expert allows the following relational operators:

= equal
< less than
<= less than or equal
> greater than
>= greater than or equal
<> not equal

A **logical operator**, either AND or OR, can be used to combine two conditions. For example, *if stain = catsup AND fabric <> cotton*. We will see more examples of how logical operators can be used in a later lesson.

The rule conclusion begins with the keyword THEN and must be followed by at least one equation assigning a value to a variable. In our rule, for example, the conclusion is *solvent = dry_cleaning_fluid*. *Solvent* is the variable to which the value *dry_cleaning_fluid* will be assigned if the rule premise is true.

Note the use of underscore characters in value and variable names. Since blanks cannot be used within names, underscores are used to make multiword names more readable.

Finally, each rule must end with a semicolon. Now, press **Enter** and enter the other two rules of our knowledge base:

```
RULE 2
IF   stain = coffee
THEN solvent = cool_water;

RULE 3
IF   stain = fingernail_polish
THEN solvent = acetone;
```

Your screen should look like Figure 3.8.

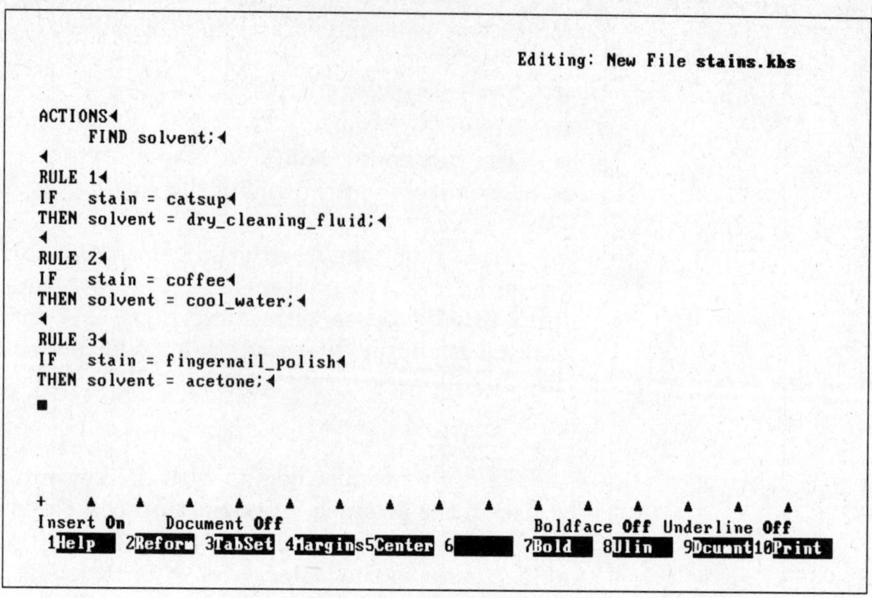

Figure 3.8 The Rules for the STAINS Knowledge Base

Step 3: Enter the Statements

VP-Expert statements ask questions, collect information, or otherwise control how the consultation session proceeds. Most statements assign characteristics or values to knowledge base variables. For example, press **Enter** and then enter the following two statements into your knowledge base:

```
ASK stain : "What caused the stain?";
CHOICES stain : catsup, coffee, fingernail_polish;
```

Your screen should now look like Figure 3.9.

Figure 3.9 A Completed Knowledge Base File

```
                                          Editing: New File stains.kbs

ACTIONS
     FIND solvent;

RULE 1
IF   stain = catsup
THEN solvent = dry_cleaning_fluid;

RULE 2
IF   stain = coffee
THEN solvent = cool_water;

RULE 3
IF   stain = fingernail_polish
THEN solvent = acetone;

ASK stain : "What caused the stain?";
CHOICES stain : catsup, coffee, fingernail_polish;

Insert On    Document Off                   Boldface Off Underline Off
 1Help  2Reform 3TabSet 4Margins5Center 6      7Bold  8Ulin  9Dcumnt10Print
```

The ASK statement presents a question to the user, whose response will be assigned to the specified variable. In this case, the variable is stain. The CHOICES statement works together with the ASK statement. It presents a list of values as a menu. Instead of having to type an answer to the question presented by the ASK statement, the user simply selects an answer from the menu presented by the CHOICES statement. The selected value will then be assigned to the specified variable, which, in this case, is *stain*.

Step 4: Save the File

Our simple knowledge base is complete. It must now be saved in the file STAINS.KBS before you can use it. Press **Alt-F6**. VP-Expert will ask:

```
Save as "stains.kbs" (Y or N)?
```

Type **y** for yes. VP-Expert will save the file STAINS.KBS on your disk and return to the Main menu.

Lesson 4: Running a Consultation

Once a knowledge base has been set up, a user can consult it to help answer a question.

Step 1: Select the Consult Option

To use the simple expert system we have created, type **c** to execute the Consult option from the Main menu.

Step 2: Enter or Select the Knowledge Base Name

After you invoke the Consult command, VP-Expert will ask

```
What is the name of the knowledge base you want to use?
```

Type **stains** and press **Enter**. VP-Expert will load the file STAINS.KBS from disk into memory. Note that you also could have loaded the file by using the Left or Right Arrow key to highlight STAINS and then pressing Enter. Your screen should now look like Figure 3.10.

Step 3: Execute the Go Command

Figure 3.10 shows three windows and the Consult menu. The top box is the consult window, which displays the questions, choices, and output of a consultation session. This is the window normally seen by the expert system's end user.

The lower left box is the rules window, which allows you to observe the activity of the VP-Expert inference engine as it works its way through the knowledge base.

The lower right box is the values window, which displays the intermediate and final values of the variables derived during the consultation. The rules window and values window are used primarily by the person creating the expert system. They allow the creator to observe and trace the logic of the system as it advises the user.

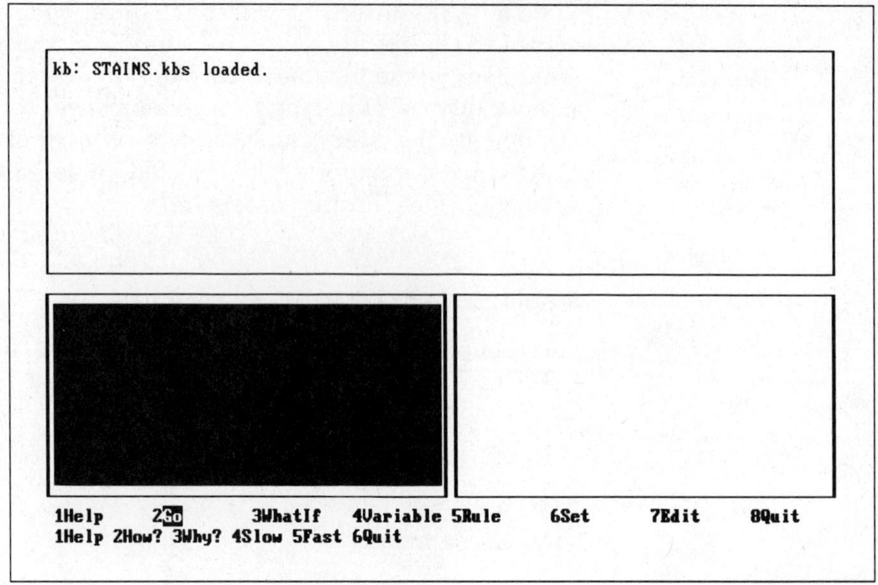

Figure 3.10 The Windows and Consult Menu

Finally, the menu listed below the rules and values windows presents the commands that are available after you execute the Consult command from the Main menu. To actually begin a consultation, type **g** or press **Enter** to execute the Go command. Your screen should now look like Figure 3.11.

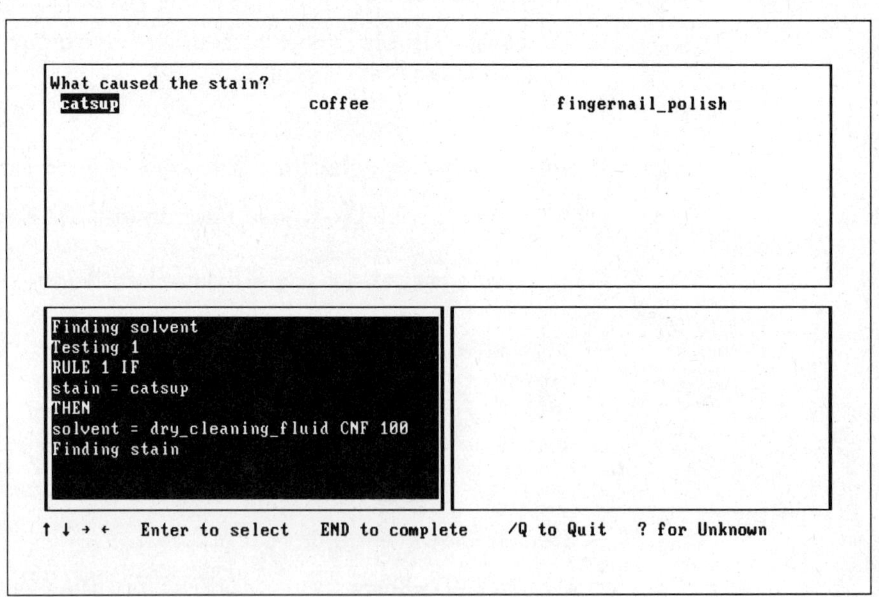

Figure 3.11 Beginning a Consultation

Step 4: Answer the Question

At this point, VP-Expert has started executing the statements in the STAINS knowledge base. The question and options you see in the consult window come from the ASK and CHOICES statements you entered into the knowledge base file. The rules window shows that VP-Expert is trying to find the solvent. It checks the first rule, but discovers that it must first determine the stain. So, the system is waiting for you to pick a stain. Press **Right Arrow** to highlight coffee and press **Enter**. VP-Expert will place an arrow beside the coffee option to indicate that this is the stain you have chosen. Press **End** to finalize your selection.

Step 5: Observe the Results

VP-Expert processes the rules of the STAINS knowledge base until it finds the answer. As Figure 3.12 shows, the results appear in the values window. If the stain is coffee, the solvent should be cool water.

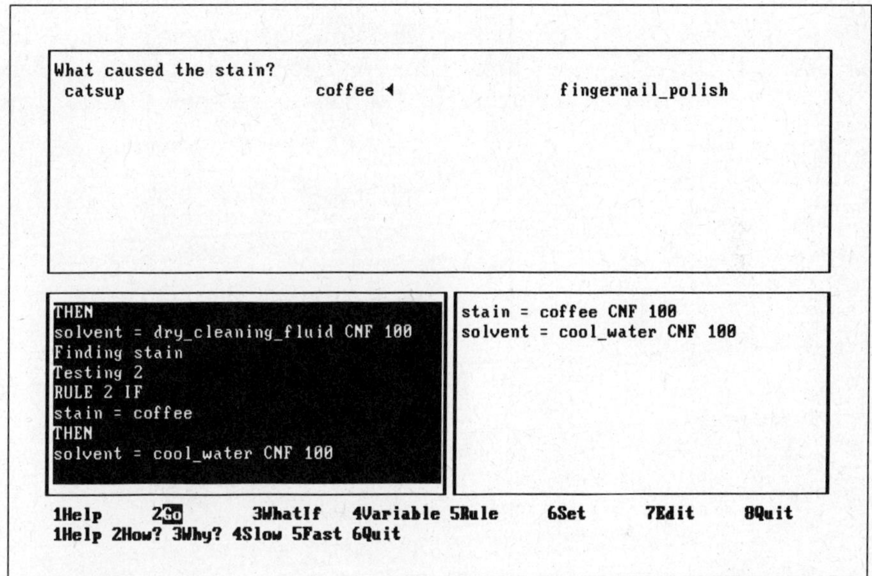

Figure 3.12 Getting an Answer from the Expert System

The abbreviation CNF 100, which appears beside each variable assignment in the values window, represents the **confidence factor**. This is a number that indicates the degree of certainty that a conclusion is valid. A confidence factor of 0 would indicate no confidence, while a factor of 100 would indicate absolute confidence. Confidence factors can be included in the rules of a knowledge base by its creator. They can also be entered by the end user when answering questions during a consultation. Confidence factors are a subjective way to assign varying levels of certainty to assertions. If no confidence factor is explicitly specified, then 100 is assumed. For example, when you picked coffee as the stain, a confidence factor of 100 was assumed because you didn't specify otherwise. Nor was a confidence factor specified when Rule 2 was entered into the knowledge base. Consequently, a confidence factor of 100 is assigned to the conclusion that cool water is the best solvent to remove a coffee stain. Whether this is actually true depends on the expertise of the person who created the knowledge base.

Step 6: Quit the Consultation

If you have other questions, you can consult the expert system again by executing the Go command. When you are finished, simply type **q** to quit the consultation and return to the VP-Expert Main menu.

Lesson 5: Demonstrating Backward Chaining

Now that you've created and used a simple knowledge base, let's briefly discuss how the VP-Expert inference engine works. It uses a problem-solving method known as backward chaining. The inference engine begins by identifying the goal variable. Then it processes the rules until a value can be assigned to the goal variable. Let's create another simple knowledge base to demonstrate backward chaining. Our new knowledge base will provide advice about the cleaning technique to use on a stain, given certain information about the substance that caused the stain.

Step 1: Create the Knowledge Base

Type **f** from the Main menu to select the FileName option. Then type **chaining** and press **Enter** to open a new knowledge base file. Type **e** to invoke the Edit option from the Main menu and enter the following knowledge base:

```
ACTIONS
     FIND technique;

RULE 1
IF   stain = set
THEN technique = soak;

RULE 2
IF   spot = dry
THEN stain = set;

RULE 3
IF   substance = crusty
THEN spot = dry;

ASK substance : "Describe the substance.";

CHOICES substance : wet, crusty, powdery;
```

Move the cursor to the beginning of the file. Check your screen to make sure it looks like Figure 3.13. Correct any mistakes you may have made. When you are finished, press **Alt-F6** and type **y** to save this knowledge base in the file CHAINING.KBS.

Step 2: Consult the Knowledge Base

Type **c** to invoke the Consult option from the Main menu. Then type **g** to select the Go option and begin the consultation. Press **Right Arrow** to highlight crusty, press **Enter** to select this answer, and then press **End** to finalize your selection. Your screen will look like Figure 3.14 when VP-Expert finishes processing your response.

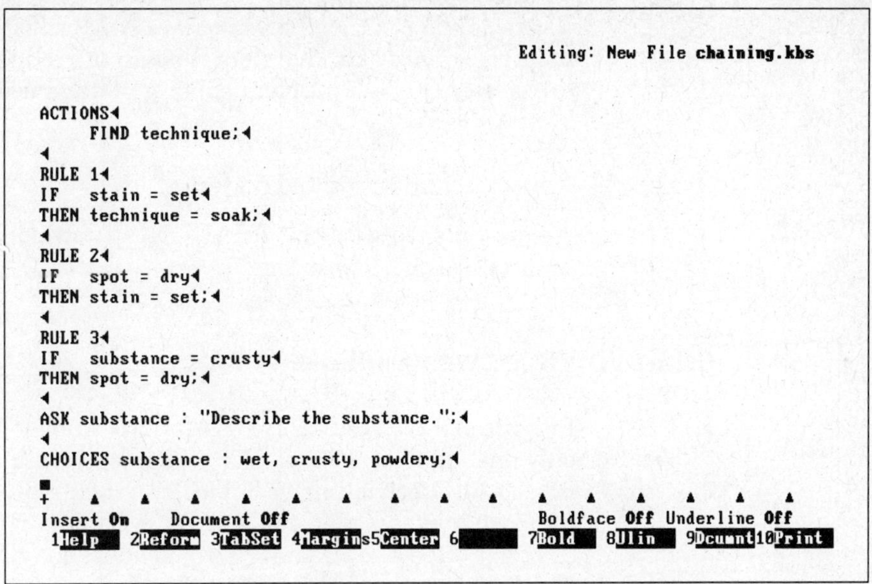

Figure 3.13 A Knowledge Base to Demonstrate Backward Chaining

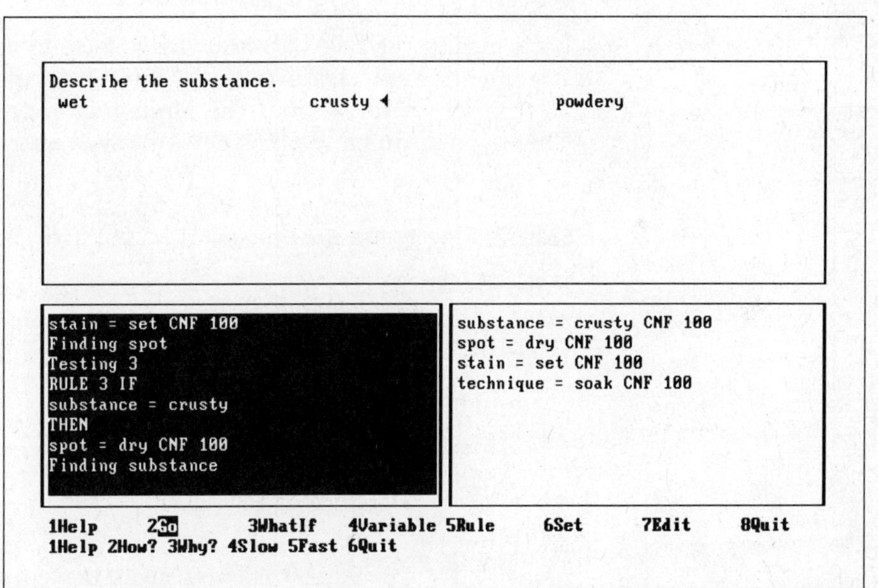

Figure 3.14 A Value Has Been Assigned to the Goal Variable

Step 3: Observe the Values Window

The values window in the lower right corner of the screen shows how VP-Expert solved the problem of which cleaning technique to use. The first rule tries to assign a value to technique, the goal variable. But a value for technique cannot be found until a value for stain is found. A value for stain cannot be found until a value for spot is found. A value for spot cannot be found until a value for substance is found. A value for substance, however, can be obtained from the user. Once the value for substance is known to be crusty, the inference engine can retrace its steps and assign *dry* to *spot*, *set* to *stain*, and *soak* to *technique*. So, backward chaining is the process of working backward through the rules, from conclusions to premises, in search of a chain of results that will satisfy the goal of the expert system. It is a problem-solving method used in many expert systems.

Step 4: Return to the Main Menu

We are finished with the CHAINING knowledge base, so press **q** for Quit to return to the VP-Expert Main menu.

Lesson 6: Using Variables with Multiple Values

In both our STAINS and CHAINING knowledge bases, each variable could have only one value at a time. For example, a stain could be either coffee or catsup, but not both. Restricting variables to single values, however, can be too simplistic. Suppose that someone spills coffee with cream on a fabric. The stain would consist of both coffee and cream. Two solvents may be required to remove such a stain. Fortunately, the VP-Expert PLURAL command lets you handle situations in which knowledge base variables must be assigned more than one value at a time.

Step 1: Load the STAINS File into the Editor

Let's modify the STAINS knowledge base to demonstrate the use of the PLURAL statement. First, retrieve the STAINS.KBS file from your disk and load it into the VP-Expert Editor. From the Main menu, type **f** to select the FileName option. Then type **stains** and press **Enter**. Type **e** to invoke the Edit option.

Step 2: Modify the STAINS Knowledge Base

Press **Down Arrow** until the cursor is on the line directly above the ASK statement. Press **Ctrl-Enter** to insert a new line. Type the following rule, pressing **Ctrl-Enter** at the end of each line:

```
RULE 4
IF   stain = cream
THEN solvent = dry_cleaning_fluid;
```

Press **Down Arrow** until the cursor is on the line with the CHOICES statement and press **Right Arrow** until the cursor is at the *f* in *fingernail_polish*. Type **cream**, and press the **Space Bar** to add the value cream as one of the possible choices for the variable stain.

Press **Home** and then **Down Arrow** to move the cursor to the line directly below the CHOICES statement. A PLURAL statement is needed to tell VP-Expert that the variables stain and solvent can each have more than one value at a time. Enter this statement:

```
PLURAL: stain, solvent;
```

Your screen should look like Figure 3.15. Note that now the entire knowledge base cannot fit on the screen at once, so a few lines have scrolled off the top and are not visible. Press **Alt-F6** and then type **y** to save your modified knowledge base in the file STAINS.KBS. VP-Expert will return to the Main menu.

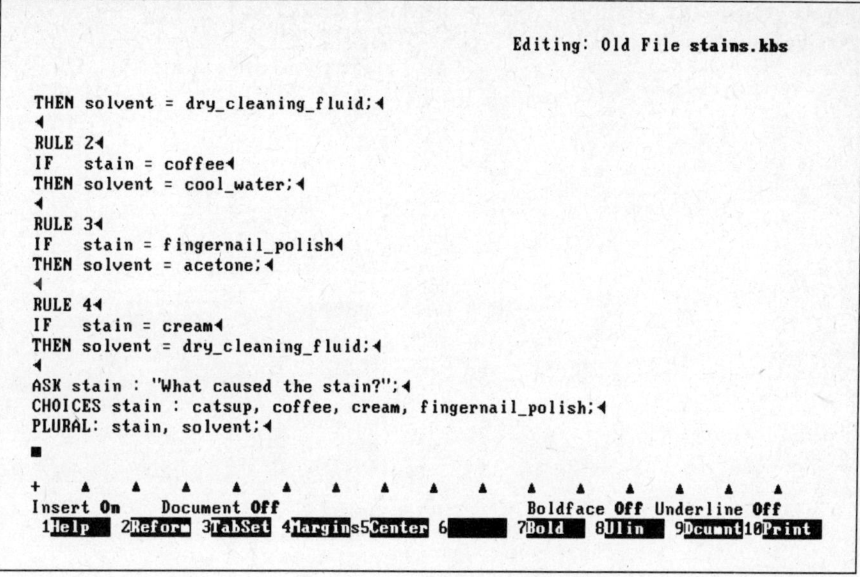

Figure 3.15 A New Rule and a PLURAL Statement Have Been Added

Step 3: Consult the STAINS Knowledge Base

Press **c** to select the Consult option from the Main menu and then press **g** to select the Go option from the Consult menu. The STAINS knowledge base will present four options for the cause of the stain. Press **Right Arrow** to highlight coffee, then press **Enter**. Press **Right Arrow** again to highlight cream, and press **Enter**. You have selected both coffee and cream as the stain. Press **End** to finalize your selections. VP-Expert will process the rules given your selections for the stain and present the results in the values window in the lower right corner of the screen (see Figure 3.16). As you can see, if the stain is made up of both coffee and cream, the knowledge base suggests two solvents: cool water and dry cleaning fluid. When you are finished examining the values window, type **q** to select the Quit option and return to the Main menu.

Lesson 7: Using Rules with Multiple Conditions

The rules we have used so far have been quite simple. A value is assigned to a variable if one particular condition is true. More complex rules can be constructed, however. For example, many stubborn stains cannot be removed completely after the first treatment with a solvent. The second treatment may require soaking in another solvent. Furthermore, different solvents may be required for washable and nonwashable fabrics. Taking these factors into account requires using rules with multiple conditions.

Step 1: Load the STAINS File into the Editor

Let's make our STAINS knowledge base more complex to demonstrate how rules can have multiple conditions.

First, retrieve the STAINS.KBS file from your disk and load it into the VP-Expert Editor. From the Main menu, type **f** to select the FileName option. Then type **stains** and press **Enter**. Type **e** to invoke the Edit option.

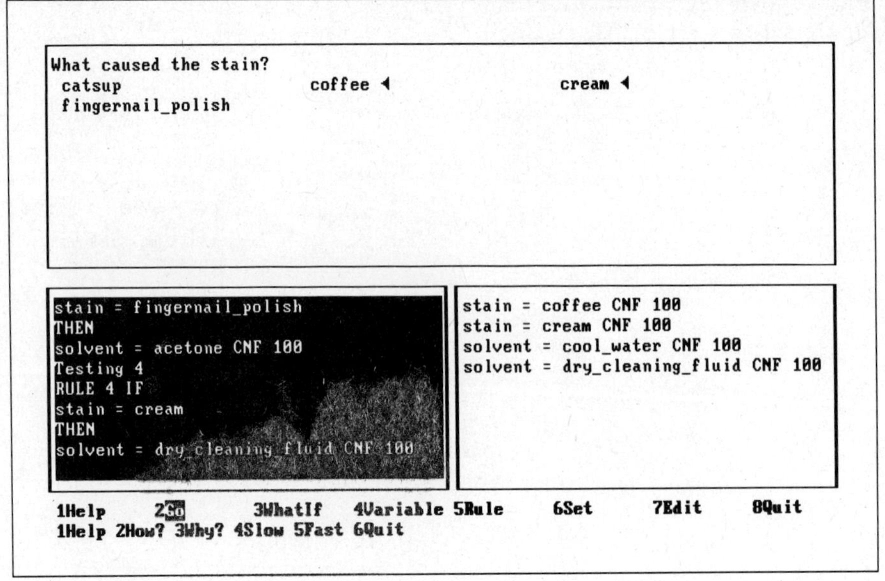

Figure 3.16 The Knowledge Base Suggests Two Solvents

Step 2: Modify the STAINS Knowledge Base

Use what you have learned about the VP-Expert Editor to change the STAINS knowledge base as follows. Review Lesson 2 or invoke the Help facility if you have forgotten how to insert, delete, and overwrite text.

```
ACTIONS
     FIND solvent;

RULE 1
IF   stain = catsup OR
     stain = cream AND
     treatment = first
THEN solvent = dry_cleaning_fluid;

RULE 2
IF   stain = coffee AND
     treatment = first
THEN solvent = cool_water;

RULE 3
IF   stain = fingernail_polish AND
     treatment = first
THEN solvent = acetone;

RULE 4
IF   stain = coffee AND
     treatment = second AND
     fabric = washable
THEN solvent = detergent_with_vinegar;

RULE 5
IF   stain = coffee AND
     treatment = second AND
     fabric = nonwashable
THEN solvent = wet_spotter_with_vinegar;
```

```
ASK stain : "What caused the stain?";
CHOICES stain : catsup, coffee, cream, fingernail_polish;

ASK treatment : "Which treatment is this?";
CHOICES treatment : first, second, third;

ASK fabric : "In which type of fabric is the stain?";
CHOICES fabric : washable, nonwashable;

PLURAL: stain, solvent;
```

Check your work carefully for typographical errors. When you are sure the file is correct, press **Alt-F6** and type **y** to save it in STAINS.KBS. VP-Expert will return to the Main menu.

Before we actually try our new knowledge base, let's discuss what we have done. Examine Rule 1. This rule says that the first treatment for catsup or cream, regardless of the fabric, is dry cleaning fluid. The logical operators OR and AND have been used to make a premise with multiple conditions. If two conditions are combined with OR, then the premise is true if either condition is true. If two conditions are combined with AND, then the premise is true only if both conditions are true. When both AND and OR are used in a rule, OR takes precedence over AND. In other words, the conditions combined with the OR are evaluated first.

Now examine Rules 4 and 5. These rules describe the second treatment for a coffee stain, which may be applied if the stain cannot be successfully removed with cool water. If the stain is in a washable fabric, the second treatment involves soaking the fabric in a mixture of detergent and vinegar. If the stain is in a nonwashable fabric, the second treatment involves soaking the fabric in a mixture of wet spotter and vinegar. Incidentally, a wet spotter is a special solution made up of one part liquid detergent, one part glycerin, and eight parts water.

The new ASK and CHOICES statements let the user specify which treatment (first, second, or third) and fabric (washable or nonwashable) are to be considered. Note that the fabric question will be asked only if necessary—in this case, only if the stain is coffee and the treatment is second.

Note also that this knowledge base is not complete. If it were actually going to be used by clients as a finished product, second and third treatments for washable and nonwashable fabrics would have to be specified in rules for all possible stains.

Step 3: Consult the STAINS Knowledge Base

Press **c** to select the Consult option from the Main menu and then press **g** to select the Go option from the Consult menu. The knowledge base will ask for the stain. Highlight coffee, press **Enter**, and then press **End**. Next the knowledge base will ask for the treatment. Select second. Finally, the knowledge base will ask for the type of fabric. Select washable. Observe the values window in the lower right corner of your screen (see Figure 3.17). It indicates that the solvent should be detergent with vinegar. (VP-Expert cuts off part of the name to fit it in the window.)

Press **g** to run the consultation again, but this time choose the second treatment with a nonwashable fabric for a coffee stain. Note how VP-Expert displays the rules as it processes them in the rules window in the lower left corner of the screen.

Press **g** to run the consultation one more time. Choose the first treatment for a coffee stain and see how the knowledge base does not ask for the type of fabric because this information is not necessary for determining the first treatment for a coffee stain. When you are finished examining the values window, type **q** to select the Quit option and return to the Main menu.

Figure 3.17 Rules with Multiple Conditions

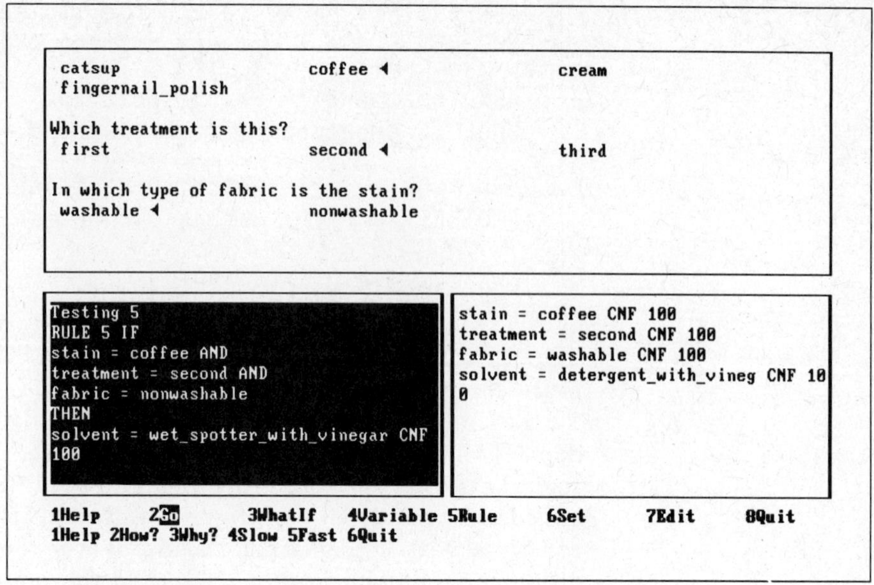

Lesson 8: Using Induction to Create a Knowledge Base

Our STAINS knowledge base has only a few rules. To be a truly useful expert system, however, it would need perhaps hundreds of similar rules. Entering that many rules would be very tedious. Fortunately, VP-Expert can automatically generate a complete knowledge base from examples stored in an induction table. Induction is reasoning from particular facts to a general conclusion. So, an **induction table** is a list of facts that presents all of the possible variable values in a column-row format. Induction tables can be created with the VP-Expert Editor or with a word processing, spreadsheet, or data base management package. A knowledge base that contains a long list of facts can be created much more easily from an induction table than from entering many individual rules. As an example, let's recreate and expand our STAINS knowledge base from an induction table.

Step 1: Select the Induce Create Option

Type **i** to select the Induce option from the VP-Expert Main menu. The program displays the Induce menu shown in Figure 3.18. Type **c** to create a new induction table with the VP-Expert Editor. Then VP-Expert asks

```
What is the name of the examples file?
```

Type **stains** to open a new induction table file named STAINS.TBL. (The program will add the extension .TBL to the name.) You are automatically taken into the Editor.

Figure 3.18 The Induce Menu

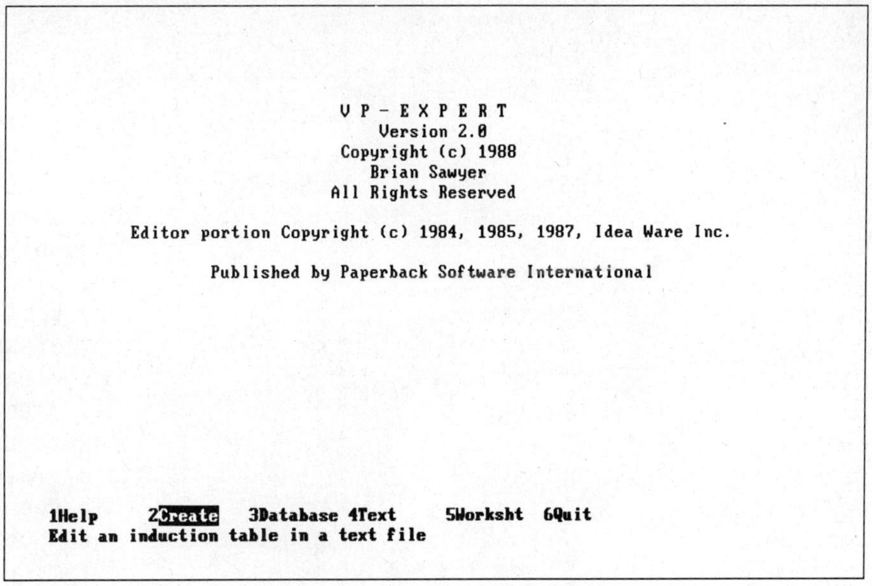

```
                     V P - E X P E R T
                        Version 2.0
                     Copyright (c) 1988
                        Brian Sawyer
                     All Rights Reserved

      Editor portion Copyright (c) 1984, 1985, 1987, Idea Ware Inc.

              Published by Paperback Software International




1Help     2Create   3Database 4Text     5Worksht  6Quit
Edit an induction table in a text file
```

Step 2: Enter the Induction Table

Each column in an induction table lists the values of a particular variable. The first row of the table lists the names of the variables. Each subsequent row in the table corresponds to a rule. An * (asterisk) in the table indicates that the value of the corresponding variable doesn't matter in that rule. Type the lines on the next page, pressing **Enter** at the end of each one. You can use the **Tab** key to line up the columns.

Check your table and correct any typographical errors you might have made. When you are sure the table is correct, press **Alt-F6** and then type **y** to save the table in the file STAINS.TBL. VP-Expert will return to the Induce menu.

Step 3: Induce the Rules

From the Induce menu, type **t** to select the Text option. This option tells VP-Expert to induce rules from the induction table to automatically create a knowledge base file. The program will ask you for the name of the examples file. Highlight STAINS and press **Enter**. Then VP-Expert will ask you for the name of the rules file to create and it will suggest STAINS.KBS. Press **Enter** to choose STAINS.KBS as the name of your knowledge base file. Using this name will overwrite your previous version of STAINS.KBS. It is all right to overwrite the old STAINS.KBS because the new STAINS.KBS created from the induction table is more comprehensive and complete. VP-Expert will take a minute to generate the knowledge base file and will then return to the Induce menu. Type **q** to return to the Main menu.

Stain	Treatment	Fabric	Solvent
Asphalt	First	*	Dry_cleaning_fluid
Asphalt	Second	*	Dry_spotter
Asphalt	Third	*	Amyl_acetate
Beer	First	*	Cool_water
Beer	Second	Washable	Detergent_with_vinegar
Beer	Second	Nonwashable	Wet_spotter_with_vinegar
Beer	Third	*	Alcohol
Butter	First	*	Dry_cleaning_fluid
Butter	Second	*	Dry_spotter
Butter	Third	*	Dry_cleaning_fluid
Catsup	First	*	Dry_cleaning_fluid
Catsup	Second	*	Detergent_with_ammonia
Catsup	Third	*	Enzyme_detergent
Coffee	First	*	Cool_water
Coffee	Second	Washable	Detergent_with_vinegar
Coffee	Second	Nonwashable	Wet_spotter_with_vinegar
Coffee	Third	*	Enzyme_detergent
Cream	First	*	Dry_cleaning_fluid
Cream	Second	*	Detergent_with_ammonia
Cream	Third	*	Enzyme_detergent
Egg_white	First	*	Cool_water
Egg_white	Second	Washable	Detergent_with_ammonia
Egg_white	Second	Nonwashable	Wet_spotter_with_ammonia
Egg_white	Third	*	Enzyme_detergent
Egg_yolk	First	*	Dry_cleaning_fluid
Egg_yolk	Second	*	Dry_spotter
Egg_yolk	Third	*	Enzyme_detergent
Fingernail_polish	First	*	Acetone
Fingernail_polish	Second	*	Dry_spotter
Fingernail_polish	Third	*	Dry_cleaning_fluid

Step 4: Consult the New STAINS Knowledge Base

From the Main menu, type **f** to select the FileName option. Then type **stains** and press **Enter** to choose your new STAINS knowledge base file. Type **c** to invoke the Consult option and then type **g** to begin the consultation. Your screen should look like Figure 3.19.

As you can see, the program asks for the value of the stain variable and then presents a menu of all the stains you specified when you created the induction table. VP-Expert automatically generated the ASK statement that presents the question above the list of stains.

Try your new STAINS knowledge base to find the solvent to use in the second treatment of an egg white stain on a washable fabric. Remember: use the arrow keys to highlight your choices, press **Enter** to make selections, and press **End** to finalize those selections. When you are finished, your screen will look like Figure 3.20. The solvent to use is detergent with ammonia.

If you like, press **g** to run another consultation and find the solvent for a different stain. When you are finished using the knowledge base, press **q** to return to the VP-Expert Main menu.

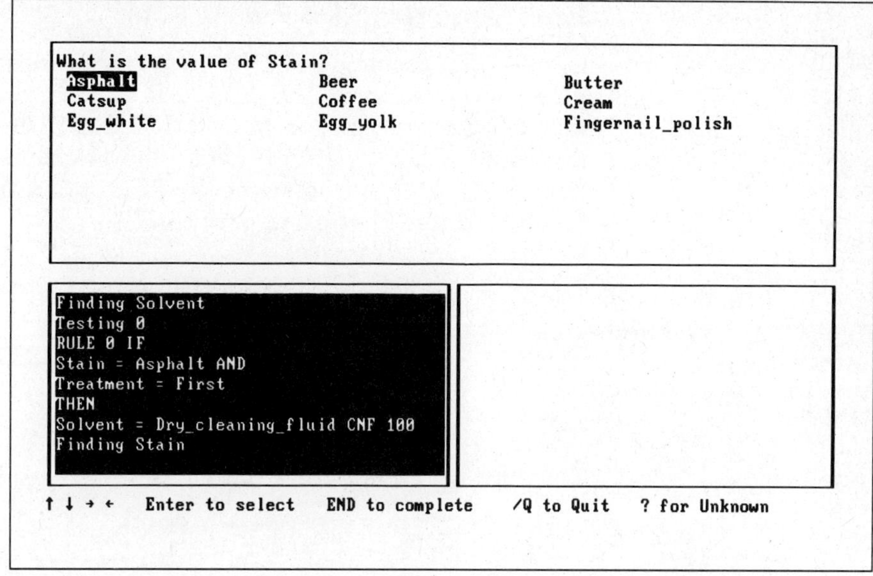

Figure 3.19 The List of Stains from the Induction Table

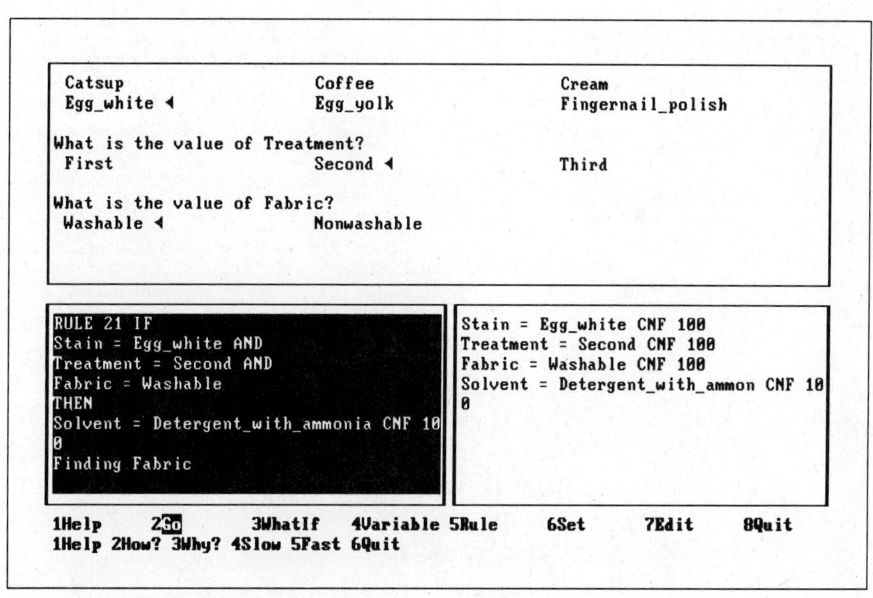

Figure 3.20 The Solvent To Use in the Second Treatment

Lesson 9: Enhancing the Appearance of the Consultation

The STAINS knowledge base you have created from the induction table is a complete, working expert system. Although it includes only a few stains, you should understand how it can be made much more comprehensive by expanding the induction table and then regenerating the knowledge base file. The appearance of the consultation, however, leaves much to be desired. It provides no conclusion message in the consultation window and it asks only generic questions of the form, "What is the value of (variable name)?" Fortunately, VP-Expert lets you easily enhance the output of a knowledge base.

Step 1: Load STAINS.KBS into the Editor

Even though the new STAINS knowledge base file was automatically generated by VP-Expert from the STAINS induction table, you can still use the Editor to modify the file. The first step is to load STAINS.KBS into the VP-Expert Editor. From the Main menu, type **f** to invoke the FileName option. Type **stains** and press **Enter**. Then type **e** to select the Edit option from the Main menu. Your screen should look like Figure 3.21.

Figure 3.21 The Stains Knowledge Base File Created from the Stains Induction Table

```
                                          Editing: Old File stains.kbs

ACTIONS◂
        FIND Solvent;◂
◂
◂
RULE 0◂
IF      Stain=Asphalt AND◂
        Treatment=First◂
THEN    Solvent=Dry_cleaning_fluid;◂
◂
RULE 1◂
IF      Stain=Asphalt AND◂
        Treatment=Second◂
THEN    Solvent=Dry_spotter;◂
◂
RULE 2◂
IF      Stain=Asphalt AND◂
        Treatment=Third◂
THEN    Solvent=Amyl_acetate;◂

+   ▲    ▲    ▲    ▲    ▲    ▲    ▲    ▲    ▲    ▲    ▲    ▲    ▲    ▲    ▲
Insert On     Document Off                       Boldface Off Underline Off
 1Help   2Reform  3TabSet 4Margins5Center 6       7Bold   8Ulin   9Dcumnt10Print
```

Step 2: Modify the ASK Statements

When VP-Expert automatically generates a knowledge base from an induction table, it creates simple ASK statements to obtain the values of unknown variables. You can usually devise more informative or explicit ASK statements. Press **Ctrl-Page Down** to move the cursor to the end of the STAINS knowledge base file. Now use what you learned about the Editor in Lesson 2 to reword the three ASK statements as follows:

```
ASK Stain : "What caused the stain?";
ASK Treatment : "Which treatment is this?";
ASK Fabric : "In which type of fabric is the stain?";
```

Press **Ctrl-Page Up** to move the cursor to the beginning of the file.

Step 3: Add DISPLAY to the ACTIONS Block

So far, you've had to look in the values window to see the results of a consultation. For example, VP-Expert might report the following conclusion:

```
Solvent = Dry_cleaning_fluid CNF 100
```

It would be better, however, to report the conclusion more clearly in the consult window. The DISPLAY clause can be used in the ACTIONS block or in rules to reveal the results of a consultation. For example, you could add the following DISPLAY clause to Rule 0:

```
RULE 0
IF   Stain=Asphalt AND
     Treatment=First
THEN Solvent=Dry_cleaning_fluid
     DISPLAY "Use dry cleaning fluid.";
```

If Rule 0 were true, then the message, "Use dry cleaning fluid," would be displayed in the consult window.

A similar DISPLAY clause at the end of each rule would present a conclusion for every possible result of the consultation. An easier way to present a conclusion for each rule is to put a single DISPLAY clause in the ACTIONS block. By adding a DISPLAY clause to the ACTIONS block, you can tell VP-Expert to report the value of the goal variable after it has been found.

Move the cursor to the semicolon after the word *solvent* in the ACTIONS block. Make sure Insert mode is turned on and press **Ctrl-Enter**. Type the following DISPLAY clause beneath the FIND clause:

```
DISPLAY "Use {#Solvent} to remove the stain."
```

Your screen should look like Figure 3.22. Note that the semicolon must now be after the last quotation mark of the DISPLAY statement. The variable name Solvent in curly brackets tells VP-Expert to display the value of Solvent in the sentence at the end of the consultation. The # character, which is optional, tells VP-Expert to present the confidence factor along with the value of Solvent.

Figure 3.22 A DISPLAY Clause Has Been Added to the ACTIONS Block

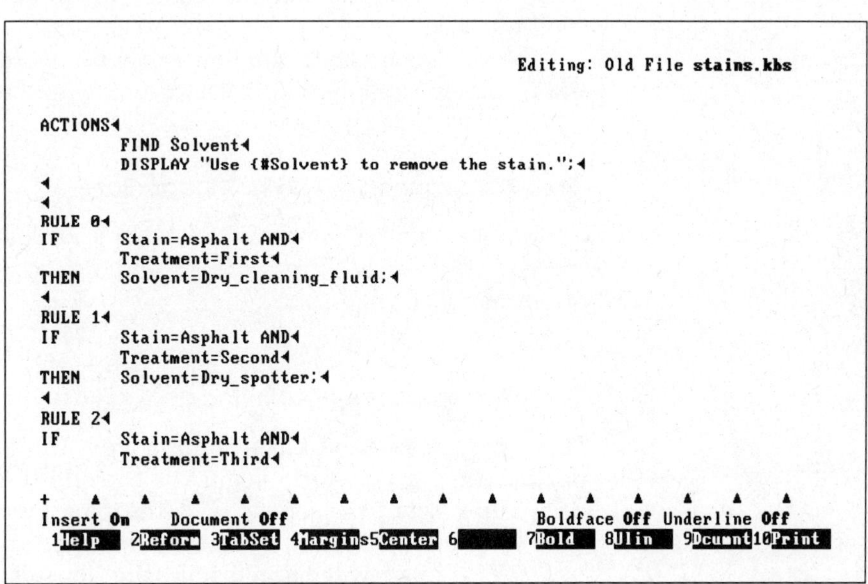

Step 4: Create a RUNTIME Consultation

By default, VP-Expert presents three windows on the screen when you run a consultation: the consult window, the rules window, and the values window. The rules and values windows are used primarily by the person developing the knowledge base to check his or her work. Usually, the end-user of an expert system need see only the consult window. After a knowledge base is complete and known to operate correctly, the rules and values windows can be eliminated with the RUNTIME statement. The consult window would then take up the entire screen, except for the Consult menu at the bottom. The RUNTIME statement can be placed anywhere within a knowledge base file; a convenient location is at the beginning, before the ACTIONS block.

Let's add a RUNTIME statement to the STAINS knowledge base. Press **Ctrl-Page Up** to move the cursor to the beginning of the file. Press **Ctrl-Enter** to insert a new line at the beginning. Press **Up Arrow** and enter the following statement:

```
RUNTIME;
```

From now on, only the consult window will appear on your screen whenever you run the STAINS knowledge base. If you want to see the rules and values windows again, you must remove the RUNTIME statement.

Step 5: Clear the Consult Window

VP-Expert provides several commands that let you control the appearance of the consult window. The CLS, or clear screen, clause is the simplest. All text in the consult window is erased whenever a CLS clause is executed. Although we don't really need one, let's put a CLS clause in the STAINS knowledge base just before the FIND clause. Then if a DISPLAY clause were added later at the beginning of the ACTIONS block, the CLS clause would clear the screen before the first question was asked.

Move the cursor to the line below the word ACTIONS. Press **Ctrl-Enter** to insert a new blank line. Press **Up Arrow** and enter **CLS**.

Step 6: Save the STAINS Knowledge Base

Before you can try your new STAINS knowledge base, you must save it in its file and exit the Editor. Press **Alt-F6** and then type **y** to save the file and return to the Main menu.

Step 7: Consult the STAINS Knowledge Base

Type **c** to select the Consult option from the Main menu. After the file has been loaded, type **g** for Go to begin the consultation. Notice how the consult window takes up most of the screen. Use the expert system to find the solvent for the second treatment of an egg white stain in a nonwashable fabric. After you get the answer, VP-Expert will again display the Consult menu and your screen will look like Figure 3.23. When you are finished examining the screen, press **q** to return to the Main menu.

Figure 3.23 The RUNTIME Consultation Session

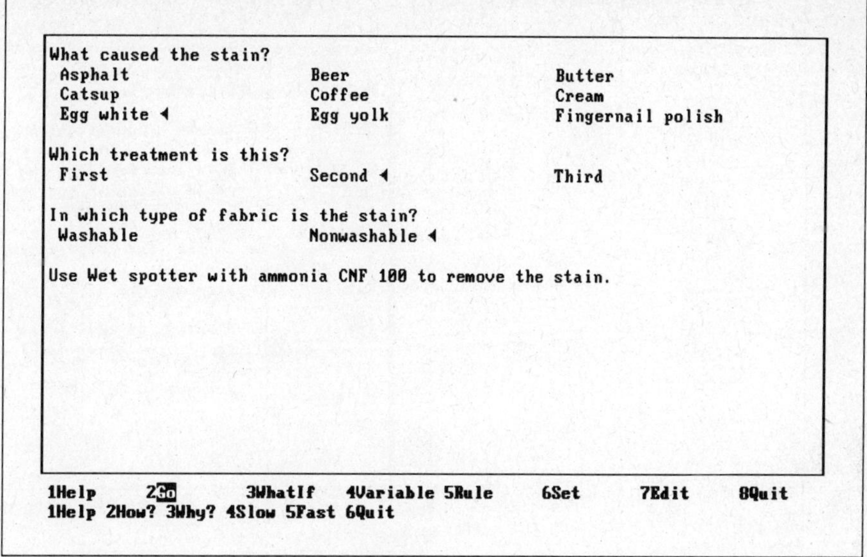

Lesson 10: Exploring the Consult Menu Options

We have used the Consult menu several times in this chapter. Let's discuss its options in more detail.

Step 1: Select the Consult Option

You should be at the VP-Expert Main menu. If STAINS.KBS is not already selected as your knowledge base file, use the FileName option to select it. Then press **c** to execute the Consult option from the VP-Expert Main menu. After the STAINS knowledge base file is loaded, the Consult menu will appear at the bottom of your screen (see Figure 3.23). Eight options are available: Help, Go, WhatIf, Variable, Rule, Set, Edit, and Quit.

Step 2: Try the Help Option

Help is the first option in the Consult menu. It is just like the Help option in all of the other menus, except that it goes directly to the help page on the Consult menu. Type **h** to invoke the Help facility from the Consult menu. As you can see from Figure 3.24, VP-Expert will present information about the options of the Consult menu. Press **Escape** twice to return to the Consult menu.

Step 3: Try the Go Option

When you select the Consult option from the Main menu, VP-Expert automatically highlights the Go option. You have already used the Go option several times to start a consultation. Notice the additional options that appear below the Go option. These are commands you can use while running a consultation. Type **g** or press **Enter** to choose the Go option. Type / (forward slash) to activate the Go menu. Six options are available: Help, How, Why, Slow, Fast, and Quit.

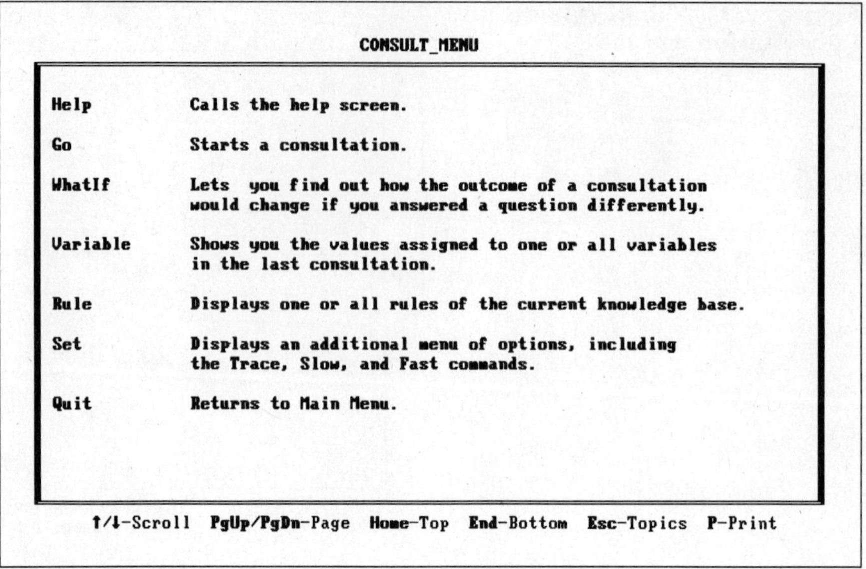

Figure 3.24 Consult Menu Help Screen

Step 4: Try the Go Help Option

Help is the first option in the Go menu. Type **h** to execute it. As you can see from Figure 3.25, VP-Expert presents information about the Go menu options. After you read the information, press **Escape** twice to return to the consultation.

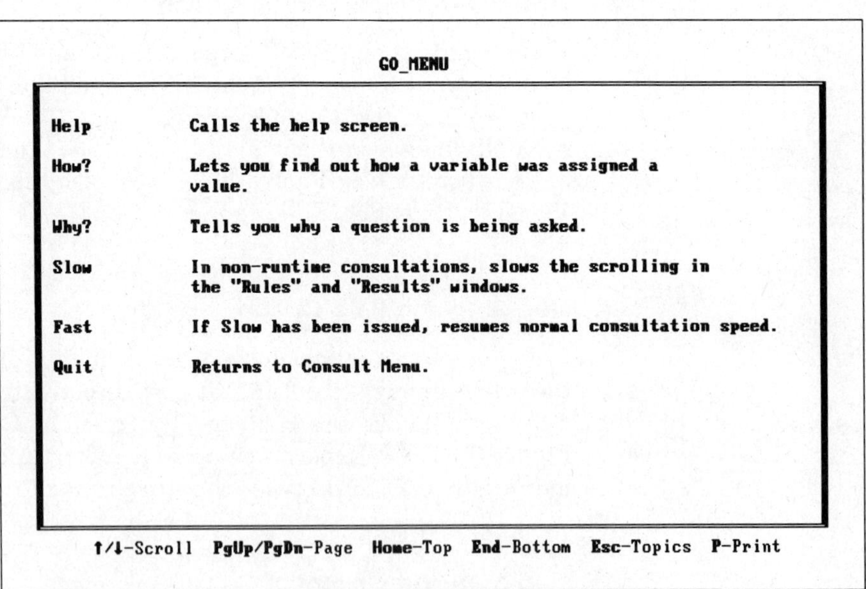

Figure 3.25 Go Menu Help Screen

Step 5: Try the Go How and Go Why Options

The How option of the Go menu can tell you how the value of a variable was found. The Why option can tell you why a particular question is being asked. Before we demonstrate these options, let's make a small modification to our STAINS knowledge base.

Type **/q** to return to the VP-Expert Main menu. Type **e** to invoke the Editor and load the STAINS.KBS file. Modify Rule 0 as follows:

```
RULE 0
IF   Stain=Asphalt AND
     Treatment=First
THEN Solvent=Dry_cleaning_fluid
BECAUSE "You must specify the substance that caused
the stain, which treatment, and, in some cases, the
type of fabric.  STAINS can then determine the
solvent that will dissolve the stain.";
```

The BECAUSE keyword is used to specify text that will be displayed on the screen during a consultation when the user selects Why from the Go menu. The BECAUSE text must be enclosed in quotes and appear at the end of the rule before the final semicolon. If your BECAUSE text takes up more than one line, leave a space at the end of each line before you press Enter or Ctrl-Enter. Ideally, you should use BECAUSE at the end of every rule. To save time and typing, however, we will just demonstrate the use of BECAUSE in Rule 0.

Press **Alt-F6** and type **y** to save the modified STAINS.KBS file. Type **c** from the Main menu to select the Consult option and then type **g** to select the Go option from the Consult menu. Highlight Asphalt, press **Enter**, and press **End** to specify the stain.

Now let's try the How option. Type / to activate the Go menu. Highlight the How option and press **Enter**. VP-Expert will ask what variable you are asking about and present a menu of variable names. Highlight Stain and press **Enter**. As Figure 3.26 shows, VP-Expert tells you that the value of the variable Stain was set by you, the user. Press any key to continue.

Figure 3.26 The How Option

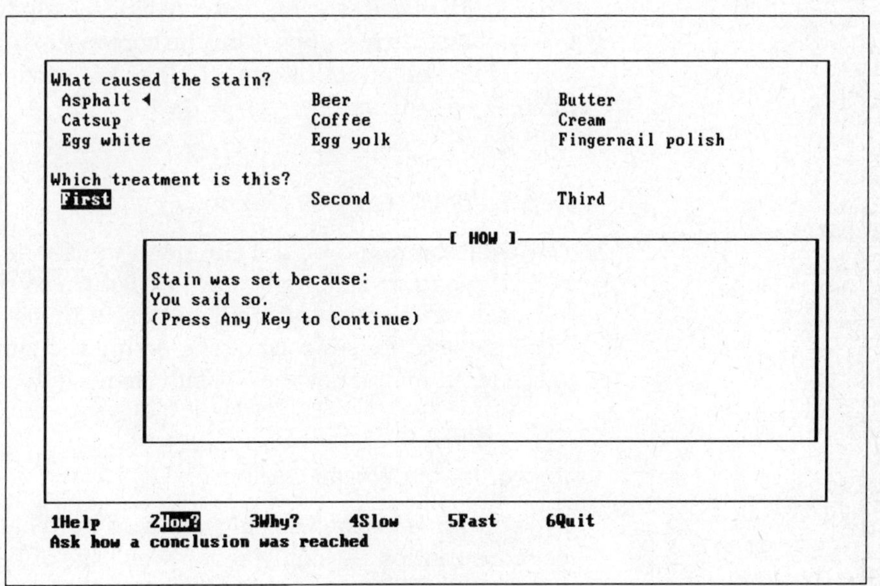

Now try the Why option by typing **/w**. Your screen should look like Figure 3.27. VP-Expert displays the explanation you provided after the BECAUSE keyword at the end of Rule 0. Press any key to continue.

Figure 3.27 The Why Option

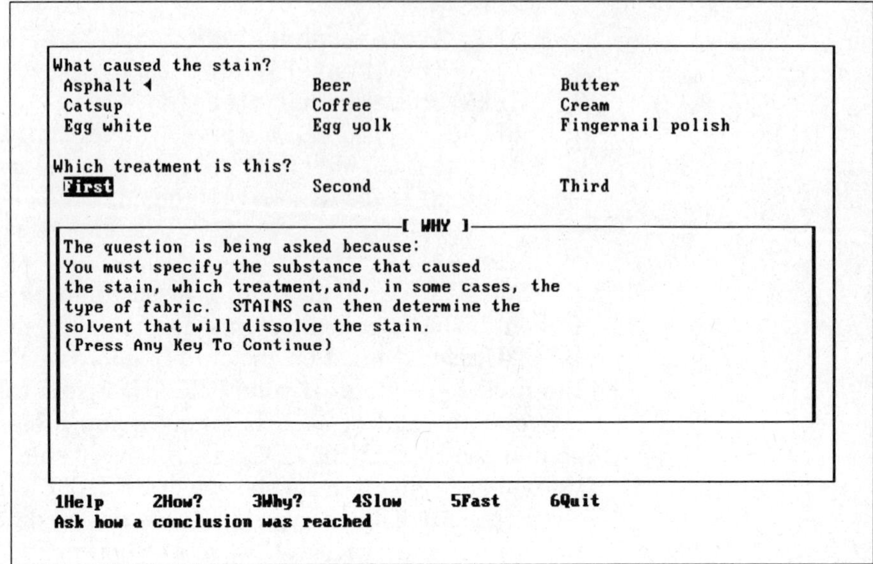

Step 6: Examine the Go Slow and Go Fast Options

Type / to activate the Go menu again. The Slow and Fast options are used to control the speed of text scrolling in the rules and values windows. These options can be helpful during the development of a knowledge base. Since we have used the RUNTIME statement in the STAINS knowledge base, however, the rules and values windows do not appear on the screen during a consultation. So, Slow and Fast would have no effect in our STAINS knowledge base unless the RUNTIME statement were removed.

Step 7: Try the Go Quit Option

The Quit command of the Go menu is used to exit a consultation before completion. Type **/q** to quit right now and return to the VP-Expert Main menu. Incidentally, the explanation of the Quit option that appears in the Go menu Help screen (see Figure 3.25) is incorrect. Selecting the Quit option from the Go menu returns to the Main menu, not the Consult menu.

Step 8: Try the WhatIf Option

Type **c** to invoke the Consult menu. The WhatIf option allows you to see how the last consultation session you ran would be affected if you had answered a question differently. To see how it works, type **g** to begin a consultation. Select Asphalt for the stain and First for the treatment. The knowledge base suggests dry cleaning fluid to remove the stain. But what if you had chosen Second for the treatment? Type **w** to invoke the WhatIf option from the Consult menu. As Figure 3.28

shows, VP-Expert asks you to select the variable you want to change. Highlight Treatment and press **Enter**. The program will then ask you to choose the treatment. This time, highlight Second, press **Enter**, and then press **End**. Now the knowledge base suggests dry spotter to remove the stain.

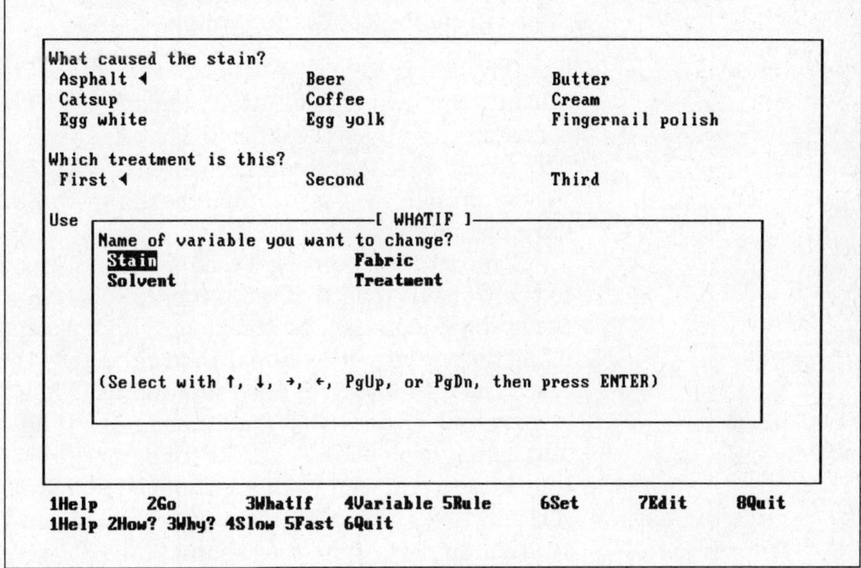

Figure 3.28 The WhatIf Option

Step 9: Try the Variable Option

The Variable option allows you to examine the values that were assigned to variables in the previous consultation. Type **v** to select the Variable option from the Consult menu. VP-Expert presents a menu of variables in this knowledge base. Highlight Stain and press **Enter**. The program clears the consult window and then reports that the value of Stain is Asphalt. It also displays the confidence factor, CNF 100.

Step 10: Examine the Rule Option

The Rule option of the Consult menu allows you to see a rule from the current knowledge base, but only if the knowledge base does not contain the RUNTIME statement. Since our STAINS knowledge base contains the RUNTIME statement, the Rule option will not work. In a non-RUNTIME knowledge base, however, selecting the Rule option presents a menu of rule names. To see a rule, you highlight its name and press the Enter key.

Step 11: Try the Set Option

The Set option of the Consult menu presents a menu of options that control certain aspects of the next consultation session you run. Type **s** to activate the Set menu. Six options are available: Help, Trace, Slow, Fast, Windows, and Quit.

The Help option displays more information about the Set menu. The Slow and Fast options are just like those in the Go menu: they control the speed of text scrolling in the rules and values windows. Slow and Fast work only for knowledge bases that do not contain the RUNTIME statement. The Windows option lets you change the sizes and locations of the rules, values, and consult windows; it works only in non-RUNTIME knowledge bases. The Quit option returns to the Consult menu. Trace is the most interesting option in the Set menu.

Step 12: Try the Set Trace Option

The Trace option causes VP-Expert to record the path the inference engine follows during your next consultation session. The Trace recording is stored in a file with the same name as the knowledge base, except that it has an extension of TRC. The result of a Trace can be viewed with the Tree option of the Main menu. The Trace option is useful for checking the logic of a knowledge base under development.

Type **t** to turn on the Trace feature. Then type **q** to return from the Set menu to the Consult menu. Type **g** for Go to begin a new consultation. Select Coffee as the stain, Second as the treatment, and Washable as the fabric. STAINS suggests using detergent with vinegar to remove the stain.

Type **q** to return to the Main menu. Then type **t** to select the Tree option. VP-Expert will present the Tree menu, which has four options: Help, Text, Graphics, and Quit. Type **t** for Text. VP-Expert will load the STAINS.TRC file into the Editor. Figure 3.29 shows the part of the text tree that you should see initially on your screen. Press **Page Down** to see the bottom part of the tree. Press **Page Up** to see the top part of the tree again.

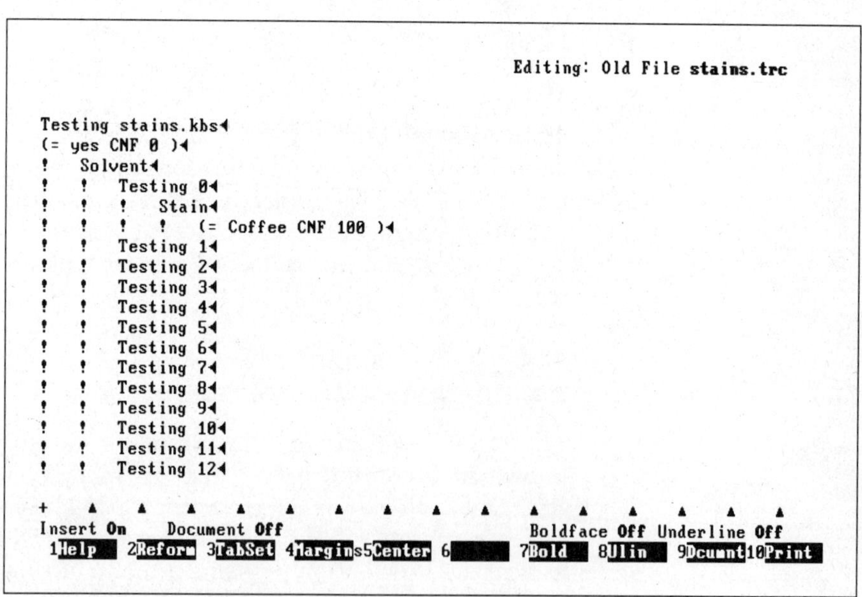

```
                                              Editing: Old File stains.trc

Testing stains.kbs◄
(= yes CNF 0 )◄
!   Solvent◄
!   !   Testing 0◄
!   !   !   Stain◄
!   !   !   !   (= Coffee CNF 100 )◄
!   !   Testing 1◄
!   !   Testing 2◄
!   !   Testing 3◄
!   !   Testing 4◄
!   !   Testing 5◄
!   !   Testing 6◄
!   !   Testing 7◄
!   !   Testing 8◄
!   !   Testing 9◄
!   !   Testing 10◄
!   !   Testing 11◄
!   !   Testing 12◄

+    ▲    ▲    ▲    ▲    ▲    ▲    ▲    ▲    ▲    ▲    ▲    ▲    ▲    ▲    ▲
Insert On     Document Off                       Boldface Off Underline Off
 1Help   2Reform  3TabSet 4Margins5Center 6       7Bold   8Ulin   9Dcumnt10Print
```

Figure 3.29 The Text Tree

Each line of this display contains one of three types of messages. The name of a variable, such as Stain, indicates that a value is being sought for that variable at that point in the consultation. The word *Testing* followed by the name of a rule indicates the rule is being tested. Text in parentheses shows a value that has been assigned to a variable. When you are finished viewing the text tree, press **Alt-F8** and then type **y** to return to the Tree menu.

If your computer is equipped with a graphics adapter and monitor, type **g** for Graphics. Press the **Space Bar** to zoom in and see a graphic view of the path taken by the inference engine. You can use the arrow keys to reveal different parts of the tree. When you are finished viewing the graphic tree, press **Escape** to return to the Tree menu. From the Tree menu, type **q** to return to the VP-Expert Main menu.

Step 13: Try the Edit Option

Type **c** from the Main menu to execute the Consult option again. Now type **e** from the Consult menu to go directly to the Editor and load the STAINS.KBS file. Having the Edit option in the Consult menu as well as the Main menu makes it easy to view, modify, or correct the knowledge base file while you try consultations. Being able to rapidly switch between the Editor and a consultation is especially convenient during the development of a new knowledge base because you can immediately test your work. Press **Alt-F8** and then type **y** to exit the editor and return to the Consult menu.

Step 14: Try the Quit Option

Although you've already used the Quit option from the Consult menu several times, try it again. Type **q** to return to the VP-Expert Main menu. We are finished with the lessons in this chapter, so type **q** again to return to DOS.

Conclusion

In this chapter, we've covered the basics of using VP-Expert to set up a simple expert system. You should now know enough about the program to create complete, working knowledge bases. Admittedly, we have not discussed many advanced capabilities of this versatile software package. For example, VP-Expert can work directly with spreadsheet packages such as VP-Planner Plus and Lotus 1-2-3, and with data base management packages such as VP-Info and dBASE III PLUS. VP-Expert can also call upon DOS commands, batch files, and other programs from within a knowledge base. Several statements are included in VP-Expert for sending output directly to the printer and for creating text windows on the display screen. We will introduce a few more of VP-Expert's capabilities in the short and long problems at the end of this chapter. If you are interested in learning more about VP-Expert, explore the built-in help facility. It contains clear descriptions of every VP-Expert feature. You can also read the well-written user manual that comes with the commercial version of VP-Expert.

Exercises

Multiple Choice

Choose the best selection to complete each statement.

______ 1. An expert system is a computer program that contains a collection of facts and a list of

(a) worksheets. (c) attributes.
(b) rules. (d) shells.

________ 2. Which component of an expert system shell uses simple logic to draw conclusions from the details of a situation?
(a) knowledge base
(b) rule base
(c) inference engine
(d) editor

________ 3. Expert systems are among the most useful and marketable products of a field known as
(a) neural network theory.
(b) fractal geometry.
(c) computer conferencing.
(d) artificial intelligence.

________ 4. LISP and PROLOG are examples of
(a) artificial intelligence programming languages.
(b) expert system shells.
(c) expert systems.
(d) heuristic algorithms.

________ 5. MYCIN, PROSPECTOR, and TAXADVISOR are examples of
(a) artificial intelligence.
(b) expert system shells.
(c) expert systems.
(d) heuristic algorithms.

________ 6. VP-Expert is
(a) an artificial intelligence programming language.
(b) an expert system shell.
(c) an expert system.
(d) a heuristic algorithm.

________ 7. What command do you enter to start VP-Expert?
(a) START
(b) VPX
(c) EXPERT
(d) VP

________ 8. Which of the following actions is *not* a way to select a VP-Expert menu option?
(a) highlight the option and press Enter
(b) type the option's first letter
(c) point to the option and double-click the mouse button
(d) type the option's number

________ 9. Which key do you press to get help in most VP-Expert menus?
(a) Enter
(b) Home
(c) Escape
(d) F1

________ 10. Which of the following terms does **not** describe one of the three basic elements of a VP-Expert knowledge base file?
(a) TYPE declarations
(b) ACTIONS block
(c) rules
(d) statements

________ 11. The goal of a VP-Expert knowledge base is expressed in the
(a) ACTIONS block.
(b) rules.
(c) statements.
(d) windows.

________ 12. The expertise of a VP-Expert knowledge base is contained in the
(a) ACTIONS block.
(b) rules.
(c) statements.
(d) windows.

________ 13. The manner in which a VP-Expert consultation session proceeds is controlled by the
(a) ACTIONS block.
(b) rules.
(c) statements.
(d) windows.

________ 14. For entering and modifying knowledge base files, VP-Expert includes a simple word processor called the
(a) Consult window.
(b) Rules window.
(c) File facility.
(d) Editor.

_______________ 15. To insert a new blank line between existing lines of text with the Editor, you move the cursor to the left edge of the screen and press
(a) Enter.
(b) Ctrl-Enter.
(c) Insert.
(d) Ctrl-Insert.

_______________ 16. A reserved word that has a special meaning to VP-Expert is called a
(a) variable.
(b) command.
(c) keyword.
(d) clause.

_______________ 17. A named storage area for holding a value is called a
(a) variable.
(b) command.
(c) keyword.
(d) clause.

_______________ 18. Which of the following clauses or statements might appear in the ACTIONS block to identify the goal of the knowledge base?
(a) RUNTIME;
(b) ASK stain : "What is the stain?";
(c) FIND solvent;
(d) IF stain = coffee THEN solvent = cool_water;

_______________ 19. Which of the following items is *not* part of a VP-Expert rule?
(a) name
(b) premise
(c) conclusion
(d) question mark

_______________ 20. A condition compares the contents of a variable to a
(a) premise.
(b) value.
(c) conclusion.
(d) relational operator.

Fill-In

1. A _______________ _______________ is a symbol specifying the type of comparison to be performed.

2. A _______________ _______________, either AND or OR, can be used to combine two conditions.

3. The ACTIONS block, every rule, and every statement must end with a _______________.

4. The _______________ statement presents a question and lets the user assign a value to a variable.

5. The CHOICES statement presents a _______________ of values to the user.

6. To use an existing knowledge base, you select the _______________ option from the VP-Expert Main menu.

7. The three boxes presented during a non-RUNTIME consultation are the consult window, rules window, and _______________ window.

8. The _______________ _______________, abbreviated CNF, is a number that indicates the degree of certainty that a conclusion is valid.

9. The VP-Expert inference engine uses a problem solving method known as _______________ _______________.

10. The _______________ statement is used to tell VP-Expert when a variable can have more than one value at a time.

11. An __________________ __________________ is a list of facts that presents all of the possible variable values in a column-row format that can be used by VP-Expert to automatically generate a complete knowledge base.

12. The file name extension __________________ is used for knowledge base files, while the extension __________________ is used for induction table files.

13. The first row of an induction table lists the names of the __________________.

14. Each row after the first one in an induction table corresponds to a __________________.

15. An __________________ character in an induction table indicates that the value of the corresponding variable doesn't matter in that rule.

16. The easiest way to present a conclusion for each rule in the Consult window is to put a single __________________ clause in the ACTIONS block.

17. The rules and values windows can be eliminated from the screen during a consultation by putting the __________________ statement into the knowledge base file.

18. The __________________ clause is used to clear the consult window.

19. The __________________ keyword is used to specify text that will be displayed on the screen during a consultation when the user selects Why from the Go menu.

20. The __________________ option from the Set menu is used to record the path of the inference engine during your next consultation session.

Short Problems

1. If you aren't already running VP-Expert, invoke the program. Use the FileName option from the Main menu to select STAINS as your current knowledge base. Use the Editor to remove the RUNTIME statement.

2. Insert the following lines in the ACTIONS block of the STAINS knowledge base before the CLS clause:

```
DISPLAY "Welcome to the STAINS Expert System!"
DISPLAY "Press any key to begin.~"
```

   Note the ~ (tilde) at the end of the second line. This character tells VP-Expert to pause when the DISPLAY clause is executed until the user presses any key. Save the updated STAINS knowledge base and return to the Main menu. Use the Consult option to try the new knowledge base. Run through a complete consultation.

3. Use the Rule option from the Consult menu to view Rule 5. Now try the Variable and the WhatIf options from the Consult menu.

4. Select the Set option from the Consult menu and then select the Slow option to make the windows scroll more slowly. Run through a complete consultation. Now use the Fast option to make the windows scroll at their normal speed again.

5. Select the Set option from the Consult menu, then select the Windows option. Try moving and changing the size of the consult, rules, or values windows. When you are finished, change the windows back to their original sizes and positions.

6. As you have seen, VP-Expert requires that you press the End key to finalize your selection of an answer to a question. If your variables can have only one value, however, you can eliminate this requirement. Select the Edit option from the Consult menu. Insert **ENDOFF;** at the beginning of the STAINS knowledge base file. Save the file and run through a complete consultation.

7. The VP-Expert BKCOLOR command lets you change the background color of your display during a consultation. For example, enter the command **BKCOLOR=7;** at the beginning of your STAINS.KBS file and then run a consultation. The number corresponds to a color, in this case, white. Try another color. Below is a list of all the available colors. Values 0 through 6 display a black background on a monochrome display.

Value	**Color**
0	Black
1	Blue
2	Green
3	Light Blue
4	Red
5	Magenta
6	Brown
7	White

8. The BKCOLOR statement lets you specify the screen's background color; the COLOR clause lets you specify the color of text or make it repeatedly blink in a rule or the ACTIONS block. You can use the COLOR clause as often as you like. If your computer is equipped with a color monitor, try the COLOR clause in the ACTIONS block of the STAINS knowledge base file. Then run a consultation to see how the text looks. Following is a list of all the available text colors, in normal and blinking modes.

Normal	**Blinking**	**Color**
0	16	Black
1	17	Blue
2	18	Green
3	19	Cyan
4	20	Red
5	21	Magenta
6	22	Brown
7	23	White
8	24	Gray
9	25	Light Blue
10	26	Light Green
11	27	Light Cyan
12	28	Light Red
13	29	Light Magenta
14	30	Yellow
15	31	Bright White

9. VP-Expert has several commands that let you use a printer for output instead of or in addition to the display screen. These commands can be convenient for creating a hard copy of the results of a consultation. If your computer is equipped with a printer, try these clauses in the ACTIONS block of your STAINS knowledge base file:

EJECT	starts a new page on the printer
PDISPLAY	like DISPLAY, but prints the message instead
PRINTON	causes DISPLAY to both display and print messages
PRINTOFF	shuts off PRINTON

10. The clauses and statements of VP-Expert are really a kind of specialized programming language. Like a programming language such as BASIC or Pascal, VP-Expert lets you insert comments into your knowledge base files. A comment consists of the ! symbol (exclamation point) followed by explanatory text on a single line. In VP-Expert, comments may be used to help explain the operation of a knowledge base; they do not affect the operation of the knowledge base. Try entering some comments into your STAINS knowledge base file. Run through a complete consultation to verify that the comments you've added do not alter the operation of the STAINS knowledge base in any way.

Long Problems

1. Use the following information to create a simple zoology expert system for determining if an animal is a mammal. A mammal is warm-blooded and has a four-chambered heart and a diaphragm for increased breathing efficiency. The body is covered with an insulating layer of hair, and the limbs are oriented vertically to lift the body off the ground. The lower jaw is composed of only one bone and the teeth are differentiated for a variety of functions. The middle ear contains three bones. The brain is large and behavior can be modified by experience. The young are born alive, except in the spiny anteater and the duck-billed platypus, which lay eggs. After birth, the young are nourished on milk from the mother.

2. Use the following information to create a simple botany expert system for determining the family of coniferous trees. If the leaf shape is scalelike, then the family of the tree is cypress. If the leaf shape is needlelike and the needles form a random pattern on the branch, then the family of the tree is pine. If the leaf shape is needlelike and the needles form two even lines on the branch and a silver band appears under the needle, then the family of the tree is pine. If the last statement is true except no silver band appears under the needle, then the family of the tree is bald cypress.

3. Use the information in Table 3.3 to create an expert system to help choose the right tools for simple household repairs.

Table 3.3 Household Repairs

Job to Be Done	Tools
cut round hole	drill, brace, saw, file, compass
cut square hole	ruler, saw, drill
fasten to masonry	drill, hammer, dowel, masonry bolts
fasten to hollow wall	drill, screwdriver, Molly bolts
fasten to wood	drill, hammer, awl, screwdriver, screws
patch hole in plaster	saw, knife, sandpaper, plaster
stop pipe leak	pipe clamp, wrench, screwdriver
replace windowpane	chisel, hammer, glazier's point, windowpane
loosen stuck window	hammer, putty knife, wax
replace switch	screwdriver, tape, switch
replace plug	cutting pliers, knife tape, plug
unclog drain	plunger, wrench, pail, lye
install lock	drill, chisel, hammer, screwdriver, lock

Hints: Use the PLURAL statement for a variable named *tools* to store the appropriate tools for the job to be done. Put a DISPLAY statement in your ACTIONS block with a message that contains {*tools*} to present a list of all the tools found. Below is an example rule:

```
RULE 1
IF   job = cut_round_hole
THEN tools = drill
     tools = brace
     tools = saw
     tools = file
     tools = compass;
```

4. Use the information in Table 3.4 on the next page and what you learned from the previous problem to create an expert system to help diagnose common automobile engine problems.

5. VP-Expert can be used to develop a stress test. A series of yes/no questions is asked. Each yes answer is worth a specific number of points, depending on the question. The points are accumulated and a final score is presented after all the questions are answered. The higher the score, the higher the stress level. Here is part of the knowledge base file to get you started:

```
ACTIONS
     DISPLAY "Are you under too much stress?"
     DISPLAY "During the past six months..."
     FIND answer1
     FIND answer2
     FIND answer3
     FIND score
     POP score, final_score
     DISPLAY "Your final score is {final_score}.";

RULE 1
IF answer1 = yes
THEN score = (20)
ELSE score = (0);

RULE 2
IF answer2 = yes
THEN score = (score + 15);

RULE 3
IF answer3 = yes
THEN score = (score + 13);

ASK answer1 : "Has your spouse died?";
CHOICES answer1 : yes, no;

ASK answer2 : "Have you become divorced or separated recently?";
CHOICES answer2 : yes, no;

ASK answer3 : "Has a close relative (other than spouse) died?";
CHOICES answer3 : yes, no;

PLURAL: score;
```

Note several aspects of this knowledge base file are different from what you've seen before. A FIND statement corresponding to each answer variable is included in the ACTIONS block to ensure that every question is asked. The score variable, which is used to accumulate the point values of each question, must be PLURAL. The first rule exhibits an ELSE clause, which is executed if the premise is false. Mathematical operations must be enclosed in parentheses. Finally, the POP command is

Table 3.4 Common Automobile Engine Problems

Problem	Possible Causes
starter does nothing	transmission in gear
	seatbelts not buckled (1974)
	battery weak or dead
	battery cables corroded
	bad starter, relay, or solenoid
starter clicks, does not turn	battery weak or dead
	battery cables corroded
	bad starter, relay, or solenoid
engine does not start	out of gas
	carburetor flooded
	poor gas vaporization
	bad ignition cables
	bad breaker points
	bad condenser
	choke plate stuck
	bad spark plugs
	bad distributor cap or rotor
	bad coil
	incorrect ignition timing
	clogged fuel filter
	dirt or water in gas
engine stalls when cold	choke plate stuck
	clogged air filter
	carburetor icing
	heat control valve stuck
	vacuum hose disconnected
	incorrect carburetor adjustment
	bad PCV system
engine stalls when hot	choke plate stuck
	clogged air filter
	vapor lock
	heat control valve stuck
	vacuum hose disconnected
	incorrect carburetor adjustment
	bad PCV system
black smoke from exhaust	choke plate stuck
	clogged air filter
	dirty carburetor
engine backfires	bad coil
	incorrect ignition timing
	incorrect carburetor adjustment
	clogged fuel filter
	dirt or water in gas
engine vibrates abnormally	internal engine damage or wear

used to put the final accumulated value of score into the variable final_score so that it can be presented with the DISPLAY clause. Using what you have learned, finish this stress test expert system by adding the following questions and point values for *yes* answers.

Have you been hospitalized? (11 points)
Have you married? (10 points)
Have you found out you are about to become a parent? (9 points)
Has there been a major change in the health of a close relative? (9 points)
Have you lost your job or retired? (9 points)
Are you experiencing difficulties in a close relationship? (8 points)
Has a new member been born or married into your immediate family? (8 points)
Has a close friend died? (8 points)
Have your finances become markedly worse or better? (8 points)
Have you changed jobs? (8 points)
Have any of your children moved from home? (6 points)
Is trouble with in-laws causing tension in your family? (6 points)
Is there anyone at home or work whom you dislike strongly? (6 points)
Do you frequently feel tense? (6 points)
Have you had an important personal success? (6 points)
Have you had jet lag at least twice? (6 points)
Have you moved or remodeled your home? (5 points)
Have you had problems at work putting your job at risk? (5 points)
Have you taken on a substantial debt or mortgage? (3 points)
Have you had a minor brush with the law, such as a traffic ticket? (2 points)

Be sure to include another DISPLAY clause to explain the final score. The higher your total score, the more stressful your life. A score below 30 reveals that you are not likely to develop a stress-related illness or injury now or in the near future. If your score is 60 or higher, the pressures on you are substantial and you may be at a higher risk for stress-related problems.

6. Develop an expert system that could be used by a travel agent for potential clients. Include questions such as the following:

   In which month(s) of the year would you like to take your vacation?
   What type of climate do you prefer? (warm, cool, no preference)
   What is your approximate weekly travel budget?
   Which three attractions are most important to you? (beach, mountains, night life, food, solitude, culture, architecture, scenery, organized activities, and so on)

   Use research and your imagination to create a working knowledge base.

7. Develop an expert system that could be used by a real estate firm to help its clients find a house. Include questions such as the following:

   In which areas are you interested? (list actual neighborhoods)
   Which features do you require in a house? (fireplace, back yard, pool, quiet street, shade trees, large kitchen, carpeting, two or more baths)
   How many bedrooms do you require?
   What is the minimum number of square feet you need?
   Do you have children in school? (none, preschool, elementary school, high school, college)
   Are you willing to repair and remodel?

   Consult a newspaper or real estate flyer for more ideas. Try to create a working knowledge base.

8. Use VP-Expert to develop a multiple-choice quiz on a subject in which you are interested. If you like, reproduce a quiz given in one of your classes. Design the knowledge base so that it explains why a response is correct or incorrect whenever the user makes a choice.

9. Develop an expert system to help diagnose IBM-compatible computer malfunctions. When an IBM-compatible computer is turned on, it runs a series of diagnostics called the power on self test (or POST). Use the POST information in Table 3.5 to develop your knowledge base.

Table 3.5 POST Information

Signal or Error Code	Malfunctioning Component
Nothing happens	Power supply or plug
Continuous beep	Power supply
Repeating short beeps	Power supply
1 long, 1 short beep	System board
1 long, 2 short beeps	Monitor
Blank screen	Monitor
BASIC interpreter appears	Disk drive A
101,121	System board
201	Random access memory chip(s)
xxxx201 and Parity Check x	Random access memory chip(s)
Parity Check x	Power supply
301, xx301	Keyboard or keyboard plug
601	Floppy disk drive
1701	Hard disk drive
1801	Expansion chassis

10. Use VP-Expert to develop a game that asks multiple-choice trivia questions in various categories and at three levels of difficulty. If you like, you can model your questions after those in the popular game Trivial Pursuit.

Appendix

Software Installation

Most operating systems and application packages must be installed on your computer before you can use them. This typically involves running a special installation or setup program included with the software. Installation programs often create a new subdirectory on your hard disk, copy the files from the floppy disks included with the package to that subdirectory, and let you specify what kind of hardware you have. At most school microcomputer labs, this has already been done for you. If you own a computer, however, you will probably have to install any new software you purchase. The documentation that comes with the software should explain, step-by-step, how to run the installation program and answer any questions that may be asked about your hardware and software. Let's briefly go over the steps necessary to install the software we discussed in this *Software Guide*: DOS and VP-Expert.

MS- and PC-DOS Version 3.30

MS-DOS 3.30 and PC-DOS 3.30 are very similar. The MS-DOS package comes with two manuals entitled *MS-DOS User's Guide* and *MS-DOS User's Reference*. The first one contains the instructions for installing the system. The package can be purchased on either 3½-inch, 720K floppy disks, or 5¼-inch, 360K floppy disks. The 5¼-inch package comes with two disks, one labeled *Startup* and the other *Operating*.

Although the DOS 3.30 Startup disk can be copied to another diskette to routinely boot up the computer from drive A, many people install the operating system on their hard disk C, if they have one. To install DOS 3.30 on a hard disk, follow these steps:

1. Insert the DOS 3.30 Startup disk into drive A.
2. Turn on the computer. If it is already on, press **Ctrl-Alt-Del** to reboot.
3. If the hard disk is not formatted (e.g., if you have a brand new computer), enter **format c: /s**. *WARNING: Do not use this command if your hard disk is already formatted, or you will lose all files stored on it.*
4. If the hard disk is already formatted with a previous version of DOS, enter **sys c:** instead of using the FORMAT command.
5. Enter **copy command.com c:** to copy the command processor to the hard disk.
6. If a subdirectory named DOS already exists on the hard disk, enter **del c:\dos*.*** to delete its contents. If such a subdirectory does not exist, enter **md c:\dos** to create it.
7. Enter **copy *.* c:\dos** to copy all the files from the Startup diskette to the DOS subdirectory on the hard disk.

8. Take the Startup diskette out of drive A, replace it with the Operating diskette, press **F3**, and press **Enter** to repeat the previous command and copy all of the files from the Operating diskette to the DOS subdirectory on the hard disk.
9. Remove the Operating diskette from drive A, store all your original DOS diskettes in a safe place, and press **Ctrl-Alt-Del** to reboot your computer from the hard disk with DOS 3.30.
10. Enter path **c:\;c:\dos;** to set up the search paths for the root directory and the DOS subdirectory. You can add other search paths on the end of this command if you like. Ideally, this path command should be put in your AUTOEXEC.BAT file (see Chapter 2, Lesson 18).

IBM DOS Version 4.00

The DOS 4.00 package comes with two short manuals entitled *Getting Started with Disk Operating System Version 4.00* and *Using Disk Operating System Version 4.00*. The first one contains the instructions for installing the system. The package can be purchased on either 3½-inch, 720K floppy disks, or 5¼-inch, 360K floppy disks. You should get the package with disks that match your floppy drive A. The 3½-inch package comes with two disks, one labeled *Install* and the other *Operating*. The 5¼-inch package comes with five disks labeled *Install*, *Select*, *Operating 1*, *Operating 2*, and *Operating 3*.

Although DOS 4.00 can be installed on floppy disks to boot up the computer from drive A, most people install the operating system on their hard disk C, if they have one. To install DOS 4.00 on a hard disk, follow these steps:

1. Insert the DOS 4.00 Install disk into drive A.
2. Turn on the computer. If it is already on, press **Ctrl-Alt-Del** to reboot.
3. After the copyright screen appears, press **Enter** and follow the instructions given by the installation program, which is called Select.
4. When you are finished with the installation program, remove the DOS floppy disk from drive A, store all your DOS disks in a safe place, and press **Ctrl-Alt-Del** to reboot your computer from the hard disk with DOS 4.00.

VP-Expert Version 2.0

When you purchase VP-Expert Version 2.0, you get a softcover manual and two 5¼-inch diskettes. One disk is entitled *Sample Files*; the other one, which has the serial number stamped on the label, is the *Program Disk*.

To install VP-Expert on a hard disk, follow these steps:

1. Turn on your computer and boot up DOS.
2. Type **md \vpexpert** and press **Enter** to create a new subdirectory named VPEXPERT on your hard disk.
3. Type **cd \vpexpert** and press **Enter** to switch to the subdirectory you've just created.
4. Insert the Program disk into drive A.
5. Type **copy a:*.*** and press **Enter**.
6. After the contents of the floppy disk have been copied into the VPEXPERT subdirectory, remove the disk from drive A.
7. Repeat Steps 4 through 6 for the Sample Files disk.
8. Put your original VP-Expert floppy disks away in a safe place.

Glossary

adapter (also called an **expansion card**) a circuit board that connects a microcomputer to some external input or output device.

application package a program that enables a computer to accomplish useful tasks.

archive attribute a file attribute that is turned on when the file has been changed since the last time it was backed up.

artificial intelligence a field of study combining aspects of computer science, mathematics, philosophy, psychology, and linguistics; the main goal of which is to enable computers to mimic certain aspects of human learning and decision-making.

ASCII American Standard Code for Information Interchange; the code used by most microcomputers for storing text in binary form.

auto-hyphenation a feature of some word processors that hyphenates words in a document when necessary; these hyphens may disappear if the document is reformatted.

bit the basic unit of data processing; 0 or 1, off or on.

block any section of text, from a single character to a whole document, that can be marked and treated as a single entity.

boot up to load the operating system into a computer's primary memory and begin its execution.

browse to skim through the records of a data base.

bug an error or problem in a computer program.

bus a set of wires and connectors that links the CPU to memory and other computer components.

byte a contiguous group of eight bits; the amount of memory it takes to store a single character.

cell the unit formed by the intersection of one row and one column in a spreadsheet.

cell pointer in a spreadsheet program, the highlighted bar that marks your current location in a spreadsheet.

character any single letter, number, punctuation mark, or symbol. It is important to note that the computer interprets spaces as characters also.

chip see *integrated circuit chip*.

clause in VP-Expert, an instruction that makes up part of the ACTIONS block or a rule.

code page a conversion table that tells DOS how to translate data stored as numeric values into letters, numbers, punctuation, and other symbols to be displayed or printed.

color graphics monitor a monitor that can display both text and graphics in more than one color.

command processor the program in an operating system that translates and acts on the commands entered by the user.

computer an electronic device that performs calculations and processes data into information.

condition an expression that compares the contents of a variable to a value.

confidence factor a number that indicates the degree of certainty that a conclusion is valid.

control panel lines at the top or bottom of the screen used to display information, messages, menu choices, and prompts.

CPU central processing unit; the part of a computer that performs control operations, calculations, and logic.

cursor a small, blinking underscore or box that marks the position where characters appear on the screen when typed.

cut and paste the process of marking a block of text and moving it from one location in a document file to another location.

daisy-wheel printer a printer with solid, raised characters embossed on the ends of little arms arranged like the spokes of a wheel; for producing slow, but letter-quality output.

data numbers, text, pictures, sounds that are to be processed into information.

data base an organized collection of one or more files of related data.

data base management package software that lets you create, add to, delete from, update, rearrange, select from, print out, and otherwise administer data files such as mailing lists and inventories.

debug to remove the bugs from an imperfect computer program.

default the predefined settings for certain features (margins, line spacing, column widths, etc.) that a software package uses automatically when alternate settings have not been explicitly established.

delete to remove, erase, or destroy one or more pieces of information.

desk accessory a utility program that provides commonly used desk functions such as a calculator, calendar, or address book.

desktop publishing the use of a computer and laser printer to produce near-typeset quality documents.

device controller a set of chips or a circuit board that operates a piece of computer equipment such as a disk drive, display, keyboard, mouse, or printer.

device driver a file in an operating system that contains the programming code needed to attach and use some special devices.

directory a list of the files stored on a disk; another term for subdirectory.

disk a medium, consisting of one or more flat surfaces on which bits are usually recorded magnetically, used by computers to store information.

disk buffer an area of memory that DOS uses to temporarily hold data being read from or written to a disk.

disk drive a computer system component that reads and writes programs and data on disks.

diskette a floppy disk.

display output screen on which the computer presents text and graphic images; monitor.

display adapter a circuit board or set of chips that controls a monitor.

document the paper output of a word processor.

documentation the user manual or technical information about a computer or software package.

document file a collection of text created by a word processing program in such a way that the text includes embedded formatting codes.

DOS disk operating system; an operating system that is stored on a disk.

DOS shell a program that enhances PC-DOS or MS-DOS.

dot-matrix printer a common type of printer that constructs character images by repeatedly striking pins against the ribbon and paper.

draft mode the fastest print mode, in which low-quality characters are formed by a single pass of the printhead.

edit to make changes to a file.

expansion board a circuit board that plugs into an expansion slot.

expansion slot an internal connector that extends a computer's bus and accepts an additional circuit board.

expert system a computer program that contains a collection of facts and a list of rules for making inferences about those facts; used to advise, analyze, categorize, diagnose, explain, identify, interpret, and teach.

expert system shell an application package that contains everything needed to create an expert system and is easier to use than a programming language such as LISP or PROLOG.

export to produce a file with one software package that is ultimately to be used by some other software package.

field a group of related characters in a data base record.

file a collection of information stored on a disk and loaded into primary memory when needed by a program; in a data base, a group of related records.

file attribute a characteristic of a DOS file such as *read-only* or *archive*.

file locking a feature of DOS that allows only one person to use a file or part of a file at a time.

file sharing a feature of DOS that allows two or more people to use the same file at the same time.

filter a program that accepts data as input, processes them in some way, then outputs them in a different form.

floppy disk an inexpensive, flexible magnetic medium for storing computer programs and data.

floppy disk drive a disk drive that accepts floppy disks.

formula in a spreadsheet, an expression that performs some calculations and is stored in a cell.

function in a spreadsheet, a predefined formula that lets you perform a useful operation with a minimum of typing.

function keys on an IBM-compatible computer, the keys on the left side or top of the keyboard labeled F1 through F10 or F12. Such keys are usually used to perform common operations with different software packages.

global pertaining to or acting upon an entire document, spreadsheet, or data base file.

graphics any kind of graphs, plots, drawings, and other images not restricted to text characters.

hard disk a high-capacity, completely-enclosed, rigid magnetic medium for storing computer programs and data.

hard disk drive a disk drive that contains one or more hard disks.

hard hyphen a hyphen inserted into a document by the user that remains in the document even after it has been reformatted.

hard page break a division between two pages in a document, manually generated by the user, that remains in the document even after it has been reformatted.

hard return a new line or paragraph in a document, manually generated by the user, that remains in the document even after it has been reformatted.

hard spaces spaces in a document, manually inserted by the user, that remain even after the document has been reformatted.

hardware the physical components of a computer system.

hypertext software that lets you store and retrieve all kinds of information in a nonsequential manner.

IBM-compatible any computer that works like a comparable IBM model and can run the same software.

import to use a file in one software package that was originally produced in another software package.

incremental backup the process of backing up only those files that have been added or modified since the last backup.

index to arrange a list of record numbers in some particular order.

induction table a list of facts that presents all of the possible variable values in a column-row format.

information a more organized and useful form of input data.

ink-jet printer a printer with a mechanism for squirting tiny droplets of ink to form text and graphics on paper.

input any data or information entered into a computer.

integrated circuit chip a thin slice of semiconductor material, such as pure silicon crystal, impregnated with carefully selected impurities; commonly used in computers and many other electronic devices.

integrated software a package that combines word processing, spreadsheet, data base management, communications, and graphics applications.

K the abbreviation for kilobyte; 1K = 1024 bytes.

key a field used to sort or index the records of a data base.

keyboard the device with which you type input into the computer.

keyword in VP-Expert, a reserved word that has a special meaning to the package and cannot be used to name variables or values.

label in an operating system, a word that marks the place in a batch file where a GOTO command is to branch to.

label in a spreadsheet, a text entry in a cell.

label-prefix character in a spreadsheet, a symbol that explicitly indicates that the succeeding text is to be treated as a label.

laser printer a high-quality printer that uses tightly-focused beams of light to transfer images to paper.

letter-quality like the output of a good electric typewriter.

load to copy a program or data file from disk into memory.

local area network (LAN) a system in which several microcomputers are connected together so that they can share hardware, software, and data.

logical operator AND or OR, used to combine two conditions.

M the abbreviation for megabyte; 1M = 1,048,576 bytes.

macro a sequence of keystrokes that can be entered, named, and replayed.

magnetic disk a semi-permanent storage medium that can be erased and written over and over again.

memory the part of the computer that stores programs and data temporarily.

menu a list of options available in a program.

microcomputer a small computer that uses a single microprocessor chip as its central processing unit.

microprocessor a central processing unit made up of a single integrated circuit chip.

modem *mo*dulator-*dem*odulator; a device that enables a computer to transmit and receive programs and data over ordinary phone lines.

monitor a computer display screen.

monochrome graphics monitor a single-color screen that can display both text and graphics.

monochrome text monitor a single-color screen that displays sharply-defined characters, but no graphics.

motherboard the main circuit board of a computer.

mouse an input device consisting of a small box with one or more buttons that is slid across the table top and allows the user to manipulate objects on the screen and select menu options.

NLQ near letter quality; a dot-matrix print mode that produces attractive output by having the printhead make two or more passes over each character.

numeric keypad on an IBM-compatible computer, the area on the right side of the keyboard arranged like the number keys on a calculator.

on-line connected to and controlled by the computer.

on-line reference a program such as a spelling checker, thesaurus, or user manual that you can use while running another program.

operating system the software that controls and supports a computer system's hardware.

output any information produced by the computer; the computer's responses to a user's input.

page break a location in a document file where a new page is to begin.

page layout software a program that lets you combine the output of a word processor and graphics program to produce documents on a laser printer.

partition a section of a hard disk that contains an operating system.

personal computer a microcomputer.

piping a feature of DOS, symbolized by the | (vertical bar), that allows the user to take the output of one command that would normally go to the display screen and feed it as input to another command.

pixel picture element; a tiny dot on a computer display.

primary memory where a computer stores the programs and data it is currently using.

printer a device for producing computer output on paper.

program a sequence of step-by-step instructions that run a computer.

programmer a person who creates computer programs.

programming language a set of symbols and rules to direct the operations of a computer.

project management package software to help you formally plan and control a complex undertaking.

prompt a symbol or statement that indicates the computer is waiting for a response from the user.

RAM Random Access Memory; the portion of a computer's primary memory used to store programs and data temporarily; also known as read/write memory.

range in a spreadsheet, a designation of contiguous cells.

read-only attribute a file attribute that, when turned on, prevents a file from being changed or deleted.

record a set of related fields in a data base.

redirection a feature of DOS, symbolized by >, <, >>, that allows you to send the output of a command to some other program or output device.

relational data base a data base that is organized in two-dimensional tables of rows (records) and columns (fields).

relational operator a symbol specifying the type of comparison to be performed, such as =, <, >, <=, >=, or <>.

replaceable parameter a feature of DOS that allows the user to pass information to a batch file while it is running.

resolution the sharpness of a display screen.

right justification aligning text to the right margin.

ROM Read Only Memory; permanent primary storage that is encoded with programs and data at the factory, and can be read and used, but never erased, changed, or augmented, by the user.

scroll to shift what is on a computer display screen so that other areas are visible.

soft page break a division between two pages in a document that is automatically generated by a word processor; may be changed if the document is reformatted.

soft return a new line or paragraph in a document that is automatically generated by a word processor; may be changed if the document is reformatted.

soft spaces spaces between words in a document that are generated by a word processor to justify text in a document; may be changed if the document is reformatted.

software a program or set of programs that tells a computer system what to do.

software integration the sharing of data files between different software packages.

sort to arrange the records of a data base in some particular order.

spreadsheet a table of columns and rows of numbers, text labels, and formulas used in an electronic spreadsheet package for the manipulation of numerical, financial, and accounting data.

spreadsheet package software that lets you manipulate spreadsheets.

system board the main circuit board of a computer.

system software the software that handles the many details of managing a computer system.

system unit in IBM-compatible computers, the box that contains the central processing unit, memory, circuit boards, disk drives, and power switch for the system.

upwardly compatible an operating system or software package that adds new capabilities, yet retains all previous features.

utility a small, specific program that adds handy features to a particular operating system or application package.

variable a named storage area for holding a value.

windowing environment software that allows you to divide your screen into two or more boxes and run a separate program in each one.

word processing package a software package used to create, enter, edit, format, store, and print documents.

word wrap a word processing feature that automatically begins new lines when necessary without the user having to press the Enter key (carriage return).

Answers to Exercises

Chapter 1 The Microcomputer

Multiple Choice

1. c	6. c	11. a	16. c
2. a	7. c	12. b	17. d
3. d	8. b	13. a	18. c
4. b	9. a	14. b	19. b
5. a	10. d	15. d	20. c

Fill-In

1. IBM-compatible
2. processing
3. hardware
4. bus
5. RAM, ROM
6. hard disk drives
7. pixels
8. VGA
9. mouse
10. cursor
11. dot-matrix
12. software
13. languages
14. application
15. graphics
16. desktop publishing or page layout
17. integrated
18. windowing
19. project
20. expert

Chapter 2 The PC-DOS Operating System

Multiple Choice

1. c	6. a	11. d	16. a
2. b	7. c	12. b	17. b
3. a	8. c	13. c	18. d
4. d	9. b	14. d	19. c
5. d	10. a	15. b	20. a

Fill-In

1. files
2. PC-DOS, MS-DOS
3. memory
4. date, time
5. DIR
6. eight
7. classify
8. Escape or Esc
9. Ctrl-Break
10. prompt
11. CHKDSK
12. formatted
13. COPY
14. global
15. format
16. rename
17. ERASE or DEL
18. text
19. PRINT
20. MD or MKDIR, CD or CHDIR, RD or RMDIR

Chapter 3 Expert Systems: VP-Expert

Multiple Choice

1. b
2. c
3. d
4. a
5. c
6. b
7. b
8. c
9. d
10. a
11. a
12. b
13. c
14. d
15. b
16. c
17. a
18. c
19. d
20. b

Fill-In

1. relational operator
2. logical operator
3. semicolon
4. ASK
5. menu
6. Consult
7. values
8. confidence factor
9. backward chaining
10. PLURAL
11. induction table
12. KBS, TBL
13. variables
14. rule
15. asterisk (or *)
16. DISPLAY
17. RUNTIME
18. CLS
19. BECAUSE
20. Trace